Inside the Community

Inside the Community

Understanding Muslims through Their Traditions

Phil Parshall

Baker Books

A Division of Baker Book House Co
Grand Rapids, Michigan 49516

Published by Baker Books
a division of Baker Book House Company
P.O. Box 6287, Grand Rapids, MI 49516-6287

Printed in the United States of America

Library of Congress Cataloging-in-Publication Data
Parshall, Phil.
    Inside the community: understanding Muslims through their traditions / Phil Parshall.
        p. cm.
    Includes bibiliographical references.
    ISBN 0-8010-7132-1
    1. Hadith. 2. Islam—Relations—Christianity. 3. Christianity and other religions—Islam. I. Title.
    BP135.P37 1994
    296'.124106—dc20   94-2526

In memory of
John Speers,
one of my closest friends and colleagues in ministry. John was murdered on June 11, 1991, as he was engaged in sharing the gospel with Muslims. "He is no fool who gives what he cannot keep, to gain what he cannot lose" (Jim Elliot).

In Appreciation

Peter Paget
Bill Nelson
Keith Jones
George Hemming
Ed Welch
Merle Inniger
Ian Hay
Andrew Ng

Men of God used by our Lord in leadership during thirty-two years of membership in my mission. Exemplary men of courage, humility, vision, and, most particularly, patience in dealing with me. For their continual encouragement and enduring grace, I am forever indebted and overwhelmingly grateful.

Other Books by the Author

The Fortress and the Fire
New Paths in Muslim Evangelism
Bridges to Islam
Beyond the Mosque
The Cross and the Crescent

ontents

Foreword

God is turning the heart of his people around the world to the Muslims. Never in history have so many Christian leaders agreed that "now is the hour" for the church to fulfill God's purposes among the more than one billion disciples of Muhammad.

Yet so few are ready to love Muslims by trying to understand "where they are coming from." My friend and fellow missionary to the Muslims, Phil Parshall, is a challenging and stimulating exception. Once again, this prolific writer makes us face up to our shallow understanding of Islam. Once again, he asks the hard questions that God will use to bring a greater depth to the reader.

And fascinating is an understatement! Otherwise knowledgeable world Christians hardly know the Hadith exists, much less what it says. It is difficult to put down this selection of authorized biographical excerpts from the life and teaching of Muhammad.

No Christian worker who desires to be effective among Muslims can afford to be ignorant of the Hadith. Therefore, I will be distributing *Inside the Community* everywhere I go.

Dr. Greg Livingstone
Founder and Director, FRONTIERS

*I*ntroduction

*W*hat governs the actions of Muslims? Do historical, cultural, and religious dynamics combine to produce unique behavior? For many years I had missed one of the key components to the attitudes and actions of Muslims. The Traditions (Hadith) of Islam were essentially unknown to me. After my "enlightenment" I was surprised to learn that only a minority of Muslims have ever directly encountered a book of Hadith. Their information is filtered to them through their Islamic teachers and oral tradition.

Yet, Muslims are overwhelmingly affected by the Hadith, which is a record of the words and deeds of Muhammad. These sayings and deeds came to be grouped into six major collections:

Scholars sifted the vast body of sayings attributed to the Prophet and classified them according to those that were certain, doubtful, and spurious. Gradually this process produced the six major canonical collections which came to be accepted by the Sunni community. . . . These works, all compiled in the third/ninth century, received the seal of approval of the ulama and the community in the form of ijma, or consensus. They came to form an indispensable source upon which Sunni Islam has relied for over a millennium (Nasr 1987, 104–5).

11

The Quran informs the faithful, "Verily in the messenger of Allah you have a good example" (Quran 33:21). To the maximum extent possible, Muslims are to follow the precedent of the Prophet in everyday situations. These attitudes and styles of behavior have been passed on to the worldwide community of Muslims through oral and written methods for thirteen hundred years.

An excellent overview of the Hadith has been given by Ram Swarup (1983, xv–xvi):

> The Prophet is caught as it were in the ordinary acts of his life—sleeping, eating, mating, praying, hating, dispensing justice, planning expeditions and revenge against his enemies. The picture that emerges is hardly flattering, and one is left wondering why in the first instance it was reported at all and whether it was done by his admirers or enemies. One is also left to wonder how the believers, generation after generation, could have found this story so inspiring.
>
> The answer is that the believers are conditioned to look at the whole thing through the eyes of faith. An infidel in his fundamental misguidance may find the Prophet rather sensual and cruel—and certainly many of the things he did do not conform to ordinary ideas of morality—but the believers look at the whole thing differently. To them morality derives from the Prophet's actions; the moral is whatever he did. Morality does not determine the Prophet's actions, but his actions determine and define morality. Muhammad's acts were not ordinary acts; they were Allah's own acts.
>
> It was in this way and by this logic that Muhammad's opinions became the dogmas of Islam and his personal habits and idiosyncrasies became moral imperatives: Allah's commands for all believers in all ages and climes to follow.

So, an understanding of morality is to be derived from a study of the Prophet's life. Although Christians can hardly comprehend this as we find it in the Hadith, to Muslims it is a theological premise to be accepted and acted upon by faith. To question the Quran or authoritative Hadith is to insult God. Few have been so bold.

But a distinction must be made between the inerrant, mechanically dictated and totally authoritative Quran and the Hadith. Even Maurice Bucaille, a French medical doctor who converted to Islam, is forced to equivocate on a few of the Traditions that run counter to scientific realities: "The difference is in fact quite staggering between the accuracy of the data contained in the Quran, when compared with modern scientific knowledge, and the highly questionable character of certain statements in the hadiths on subjects whose tenor is essentially scientific" (Bucaille 1979, 244). Overall, however, we can conclude that Muslims accept the Hadith as truth. If there is a problem text, they either ignore it or seek to explain it away through questionable exegesis.

The Hadith texts, although ancient, are eminently readable. At places the reader will break into laughter, as when reading about Moses, naked, running after a rock that is stealing his clothes. Perplexity will come when pondering Muhammad's marital and sex life. Horror may be the reaction when jihad is described in gruesome form. But the result will be a dramatic new understanding of why Muslims think and act as they do. The ongoing influence of Muhammad in the lives of one billion people will be better understood.

As a basis for this book I have chosen the research of Abu 'Abd Allah Muhammad Al-Bukhari. His work is universally regarded as the most authoritative collection of Traditions. Never have I had a Muslim specifically deny one of Al-Bukhari's Hadith. Literally thousands of sayings of Muhammad that are in circulation today are regarded as spurious by Muslim theologians. I have studiously avoided any reference to these questionable Hadith.

Al-Bukhari was born in A.D. 811 and died at the age of sixty-five. As a boy of ten, he began studying the Hadith. His desire for knowledge became an obsession. His task was to trace oral and written accounts back through individuals for two hundred years, to the moment Muhammad spoke or acted. Al-Bukhari is reputed to have traveled extensively, ending up with a collection of 300,000 Traditions, of which he memorized 200,000. By the end of his life he had thoroughly researched 7,275 Hadith and concluded that each was an authentic record of a saying or a deed of the Prophet.

My nine-volume Arabic-English collection of Al-Bukhari's Hadith is 4,705 pages in length. I read the books twice and then chose twenty-one specific subjects to examine in this writing. It has been my desire to be fair and representative, although it has not been possible to be exhaustive. For those interested in a full exposition, I recommend they secure the nine volumes and ponder them in their entirety.

I found the collection to be much less than inerrant. There is a great deal of repetition; within the multiple renderings, one finds contradictions, omissions, and additions. There is no guide to assist the reader in making a choice as to which Hadith is authentic. In addition, hundreds of Hadith are trivial and without any clear application. I have omitted recording most of these.

Throughout this book I have interchanged "Prophet" and "Muhammad." This was done for literary smoothness and not out of a personal belief in the prophethood of Muhammad.

At places I have added notes that are the work of a translator, Dr. Muhammad Muhsin Khan. It is interesting to see how a contemporary Muslim scholar interprets some of the ancient Hadith. Infrequently I have improved the grammar of some Traditions to make them more readable. In no instance has this caused a change of meaning.

The form of citation I use for each Hadith is (9:10; 83.6.17)). Nine is the volume; 10, the page number. The book is 83, the chapter is 6, and the number of the tradition is 17. This style of citation should enable the reader to find any Hadith, no matter which Al-Bukhari collection is used.

In any references to the English Quran I have quoted from Mohammed Pickthall's *Meaning of the Glorious Koran*.

It is my opinion that it is permissible to utilize Hadith passages in witness to Muslims. This must be done with sensitivity and never in a mocking manner. Muslims will be extremely surprised, and even impressed, that you have a functional knowledge of their Hadith.

The birthing of this book has taken place in the context of my ministerial involvement with Muslims in a major Asian city. I trust this enhances to some degree the authenticity of my writings.

Recently, the front wall of my "Reading Center" was defaced by an angry Muslim who scrawled graffiti declaring me to be an infidel. Those are hurtful words. But I go on record as having a deep and constraining love for Muslims in my heart. Even though a Muslim put a bullet into the brain of my close friend and colleague, John Speers, I can still say, by God's grace, my heart is tender toward the children of Ishmael.

I would be remiss if I did not acknowledge the tremendous input of my wife, Julie, into this book. We have had the joyous and fulfilling experience of working together on six such projects along with serving the Lord as one flesh among Muslims for more than three decades.

uran

*T*he Hadith elucidates Quranic content. It also colorfully adds background to the context of Quranic revelation. Thus, the reader of the Hadith is treated to an inside glimpse behind the dynamics of Quranic authorship and contextual realities.

Throughout history, Islamic scholars have debated the actual nature of the Quran:

> [Translator's Note: Some Islamic sects such as Mutazila and others, believe that the Quran is created, but Bukhari and the Muslims of the first three centuries of Islam believe that the Quran is a quality of Allah (like seeing, hearing, knowing) and not created] (9:427; 93.32.572).

Orthodox Islam generally affirms the uncreated Quran. Allah was and is preexistent to everything known and unknown. His Word is an integral part of his being. It could no more be created than Allah himself could be created.

Yet this affirmation presents an empirical problem. At a precise point in time and space the Quran was revealed, recited, recorded, and spread to multitudes. Prior to A.D. 610, not one word of the Quran was known to mankind and, according to Muslim belief, not one syllable of Allah's revelation was uttered following the demise of Muhammad in 632. Do we not see specific time perimeters in this revelatory process? Muslims respond that the twenty-two years was simply a telling forth of that which always was. Within the very being of eternal Allah and coexistent with his essence was his Word.

At this theological point there is congruence between the Quran and Jesus Christ. Jesus was without beginning, one with God Almighty. Yet, two thousand years ago there was an identifiable moment of birth and revelation. Muslims struggle deeply, seeking to understand this Christian view of an incarnation of God. But does not Islam also teach an incarnation of God as a written word? John 1 carries the analogy further with the assertion that Jesus is and was the Word of God. This truth can be explored further with our Muslim friends as a potential theological bridge of understanding.

Inspiration of the Quran

The Quran simply sets forth its existence as ultimate truth. The mechanics of revelation are not internally defined. We look to the Hadith for an amplification of detail.

There are some interesting parallels between the early spiritual struggles of Moses and the hesitancy of Muhammad in responding to the call of Allah, as the record of Muhammad's first encounter with the angel Gabriel shows:

> Narrated Aisha: Truth descended upon him (Muhammad) while he was in the cave of Hira. The angel came to him in it and asked him to read. The Prophet replied, "I do not know how to read." (The Prophet added), "The angel caught me (forcefully) and pressed me so hard that I could not bear it anymore. He then released me and again asked me to read, and I replied, 'I do not know how to read,' whereupon he caught me again and pressed me a second time till I could not bear it anymore. He then released me and asked me again to read, but again I replied, 'I do not know how to read (or, what shall I read?).' Thereupon he caught me for the third time and pressed me and then released me and said, 'Read: In the Name of your Lord, Who has created (all that exists). He has created man from a clot. Read and Your Lord is Most Generous that which he knew not.'" (Quran 96:1–5). Then Allah's Apostle returned with the Inspiration, his neck muscles twitching with

terror till he entered upon Khadija (Muhammad's first wife) and said, "Cover me! Cover me!" They covered him till his fear was over and then he said, "O Khadija, what is wrong with me?" Then he told her everything that had happened and said, "I fear that something may happen to me." Khadija said, "Never! But have glad tidings, for by Allah, Allah will never disgrace you" (9:91–92; 87.1.111).

At least in this initial instance, Muhammad was said to have experienced serious psychological and even physical trauma as he was visited by a divine messenger. This is reinforced by a further Hadith that is often quoted by Muhammad's antagonists.

Narrated Aisha: "How is the Divine Inspiration revealed to you?" Allah's Apostle replied, "Sometimes it is (revealed) like the ringing of a bell, this form of inspiration is the hardest of all and then this state passes off after I have grasped what is inspired. Sometimes the Angel comes in the form of a man and talks to me and I grasp whatever he says." Aisha [Muhammad's favorite wife] added: "Verily I saw the Prophet being inspired Divinely on a very cold day and noticed the sweat dropping from his forehead (as the inspiration was over)" (1:2; 1.1.2).

What was going on in Muhammad's mind during these moments of "divine enlightenment"? Hallucinations? Epileptic fits? Demonic possession? Or, as one billion Muslims believe, a direct encounter with God, not altogether unlike Jacob had (Gen. 32)?

It is difficult to dogmatically draw conclusions on these issues. What can be said is this: Regardless of the sincerity (or otherwise) of Muhammad, the results of his receiving the Quran have positioned Islam in an antithetical relationship to Christianity. It is impossible for both the Quran and the Bible to have been fully inspired by the same God. Muhammad, at least in a human sense, was the conduit of Islamic Scripture and therefore bears responsibility for the dissonance found between the Bible and the Quran. Muslims, of course, reject this line of reasoning, affirming Muhammad as a neutral spokesperson for Allah.

The Character of Muhammad and Transmission of the Quran

A rather earthy description of Muhammad is narrated by the father of Yala bin Umaiya:

> I wished to see the Prophet being divinely inspired. Umar said to me, 'Come! Will you be pleased to look at the Prophet while Allah is inspiring him?' I replied in the affirmative. Umar lifted one corner of the cloth and I looked at the Prophet who was snoring. (The sub-narrator thought that he said, The snoring was like that of a camel) (3:10; 27.10.17).

On the other hand, Muhammad was said to have had stunning encounters with the angel Gabriel:

> Narrated Jabir bin Abdullah: The Prophet said, "The Divine Inspiration was delayed for a short period but suddenly, as I was walking, I heard a voice in the sky, and when I looked up towards the sky, to my surprise, I saw the angel who had come to me in the Hira Cave, and he was sitting on a chair in between the sky and the earth. I was so frightened by him that I fell on the ground . . . Then Allah sent the Revelation . . ." (4:303; 54.6.461).

Muhammad was never frivolous in his dealing with the divine messenger; he always directed a sense of awe and worship toward Gabriel. It is interesting to note that Gabriel was seated. There was a humanness integrated into Muhammad's perception of the other-worldly.

Muhammad's relationship with angel Gabriel was also ongoing and intimate.

> Fatima said, "The Prophet told me secretly, 'Gabriel used to recite the Quran to me and I to him once a year, but this year he recited the whole Quran with me twice'" (6:485; 61.7.518).

> Narrated Ibn Abbas: ". . . Gabriel used to meet him [Muhammad] every night in Ramadan to study the Holy Quran carefully together" (4:295; 54.6.443).

It stretches one's imagination to visualize the Prophet, perhaps sitting on a straw mat under a star-studded sky, conversing with his heavenly visitor. A number of questions arise in our minds. Did Gabriel speak Arabic? What physical form did the angel take? Did anyone else notice this unique meeting of humanity and divinity that went on for twenty-eight evenings? In response to our rational questions, the Muslim smiles and in a condescending manner replies, "With Allah all things are possible."

In the elusive quest of preparing a psychological profile of Muhammad, we are confronted with a great variety of contradictory data. At times, we see the Prophet as gentle, loving, and of joyful countenance. Conversely, moods of melancholy were known to move him to the edge of despair. Few Muslims realize Muhammad's depression led him to seriously consider suicide on more than one occasion.

Narrated Aisha: The Prophet became so sad as we have heard that he intended several times to throw himself from the tops of high mountains and everytime he went up to the top of a mountain in order to throw himself down, Gabriel would appear before him and say, "O Muhammad! You are indeed Allah's Apostle in truth," whereupon his heart would become quiet and he would calm down and would return home. And whenever the period of the coming of the inspiration became long, he would do as before, but when he used to reach the top of a mountain, Gabriel would appear before him and say to him what he had said before (9:93–94; 87.1.111).

It would seem that Muhammad's whole life focused on his interaction with Allah. His relationship with divinity was constantly reinforced through the process of receiving Quranic revelations. Any interruption was traumatic for this introspective son of the Arabian desert.

Compilation of the Quran

Compilation of Quranic fragments into one unified book was an awesome task, one that was accomplished approximately twenty years after Muhammad died. A succinct narrative of the process is preserved in the Hadith.

Narrated Zaid bin Thabit Al-Ansari, one of the scribes of the Revelation: Abu Bakr sent for me after the casualties among the warriors (of the battle) of Yamama (where a great number of Qurra
were killed). Umar was present with Abu Bakr who said, "Umar
has come to me and said, The people have suffered heavy casualties on the day of (the battle of) Yamama, and I am afraid that there
will be more casualties among the Qurra (those who know the
Quran by heart) at other places, whereby a large part of the Quran
may be lost, unless you collect it. And I am of the opinion that you
should collect the Quran." Abu Bakr added, "I said to Umar, 'How
can I do something which Allah's Apostle has not done?' Umar
said (to me) 'By Allah, it is (really) a good thing.' So Umar kept on
pressing, trying to persuade me to accept his proposal, till Allah
opened my bosom for it and I had the same opinion as Umar."
(Zaid bin Thabit added:) Umar was sitting with him (Abu Bakr)
and was not speaking. Abu Bakr said (to me), "You are a wise
young man and we do not suspect you (of telling lies or of forget-
fulness); and you used to write the Divine Inspiration for Allah's
Apostle. Therefore, look for the Quran and collect it (in one man-
uscript)." By Allah, if he (Abu Bakr) had ordered me to shift one
of the mountains (from its place) it would not have been harder
for me than what he had ordered me concerning the collection of
the Quran. I said to both of them, "How dare you do a thing which
the Prophet has not done?" But Bakr said, "By Allah, it is (really)
a good thing." So I kept on arguing with him about it till Allah
opened my bosom for that which He had opened the bosoms of
Abu Bakr and Umar. So I started locating the Quranic material
and collecting it from parchments, scapula, leaf-stalks of date palms
and from the memories of men (who knew it by heart) (6:162–63;
60.152.201).

A significant issue here is that of disciples going beyond their
teacher. If Allah had not instructed Muhammad to compile the
revelation in one set of scrolls, then how could Muhammad's followers be sure they should undertake such a task? Only God
could give them this assurance. Thus, this important record
authenticates their action as the will of Allah.

This compiler of God's revelation faced a daunting task.
Muhammad had entrusted Gabriel's words to disciples who either
carefully memorized the text or wrote the revelation on leaf stalks
and parchments. One can only speculate as to the degree of loss
of accuracy in this process. First, anything human is subject to

some degree of error, no matter the commitment to perfection. Second, human memory over a period of twenty years cannot be regarded as inerrant. Third, leaf stalks and parchments may have been the best materials in existence in Arabia during the seventh century, but errors in transcription to and from fragile materials were likely if not inevitable. The Muslim theologian vehemently denies all of these objections. He dogmatically asserts that Allah intervened in the human process and miraculously oversaw the compilation of the inerrant Quran. When we affirm minor scribal errors within existing biblical manuscripts, the Muslim only smiles and comments, "That's your problem, not ours!"

Another Hadith relates an amazing part of the process:

> Narrated Anas bin Malik: Uthman sent to every Muslim province one copy of what they had copied, and ordered that all the other Quranic materials, whether written in fragmentary manuscripts or whole copies, be burned (6:479; 61.3.510).

This extreme act of destruction—no matter if the material was original or authentic—assured a Quran not open to intricate research or higher criticism. The Quranic Council had spoken. But can we be sure these errant human beings acted within a framework of absolute inerrancy—which is what Muslims worldwide affirm? Islamic vulnerability at this point seems obvious to most Western scholars.

Problems with Quranic Authority

The Hadith, not intentionally, highlights various conflicts that surround the Quran. A representative few will be documented in this section.

Limitations of Memory

Early on, a Christian scribe dared to devalue the role of Muhammad:

> Narrated Anas: There was a Christian who embraced Islam and read Surat-al-Baqara and Al-Imran, and he used to write (the revelations) for the Prophet. Later on he returned to Christianity again and he used to say: "Muhammad knows nothing but what I have

written for him." Then Allah caused him to die, and the people buried him (5:523; 56.24.814).

The humanness of Muhammad and the limitations of his memory are mentioned a number of times in the Hadith. This is an important issue as it affects the foundational authority of the Quran. His memory is a watershed point in receiving and communicating Allah's Word. Indications are that Muhammad was flawed in this area of human faculties.

Narrated Aisha: The Prophet heard a reciter reciting the Quran in the mosque at night. The Prophet said, "May Allah bestow His Mercy on him, as he has reminded me of such-and-such verses of such-and-such surahs, which I missed!" (6:510; 61.27.562).

If Muhammad, an illiterate, did not pass on an inerrant revelation to the scribes, then it is fair to call Quranic authenticity into question.

Muhammad also forgot an event, a fact that has caused consternation down through ages of Muslim history. There is great focus on the time when Allah began revealing his Word to the Prophet. But no one knows precisely the day this occurred. This Hadith by Muhammad highlights the problem.

Narrated Abu Al-Khudri: "I have verily been shown the date of this Night (Qadr) [night in which the Quran was first revealed] but I have forgotten it" (3:131; 32.4.235).

Scriptural Abrogation

Such of our revelations as we abrogate or cause to be forgotten, we bring (in place) one better or the like thereof. Knowest thou not that Allah is able to do all things? (Quran 2:106)

The process of Quranic revelation was confined to a brief twenty-two years. It seems legitimate to ask why there should be need to cancel a text and replace it with another in such a short period of time. A few examples of abrogation illustrate the problems.

Narrated Ibn Umar: This verse:

Whether you show what is in your minds or conceal it Allah will bring you to account for it. He will forgive whom He will and He will punish whom He will. Allah is Able to do all things. (Quran 2:284)

was abrogated (6:51; 60.52.68).

Why would this verse be abrogated? There is nothing aberrant in its teaching. No indication of what verse supersedes it is given.

It has been an embarrassment that the Quran teaches that Muslims with adequate financial means can opt not to fast in the month of Ramadan, but instead simply feed a poor person each day. To mitigate such a preference for the wealthy, the Hadith states that this Scripture has been abrogated by a "verse succeeding it." It is not clear what verse this refers to.

Narrated Salama: When the Divine Revelation:

For those who can fast, they had a choice either fast, or feed a poor person every day. (Quran 2:184)

was revealed, it was permissible for one to give a ransom and give up fasting, till the verse succeeding it was revealed and abrogated it (6:27; 60.26.34).

There was a high respect for the compiled verses of the Quran. This Hadith elucidates why abrogated verses are to remain in the Quran even though they are no longer valid.

Narrated Ibn Az-Zubair: I said to Uthman bin Affan (while he was collecting the Quran) regarding the Verse:

Those of you who [are about to] die and leave wives they should bequeath unto their wives a provision for the year without turning them out, but if they go out (of their own accord) there is no sin for you in that which they do of themselves within their rights. (Quran 2:240)

"This verse was abrogated by another verse. So why should you write it? (Or leave it in the Quran)?" Uthman said, "O son of my brother! I will not shift anything from its place" (6:40–41; 60.40.53).

This next citation raises a number of perplexing problems.

> Narrated Ibn Abbas: Umar said, "I am afraid that after a long time has passed, people may say, 'We do not find the verses of the (stoning to death) in the Holy Book,' and consequently they may go astray by leaving an obligation that Allah has revealed. Lo! I confirm that the penalty of Rajam be inflicted on him who commits illegal sexual intercourse if he is already married and the crime is proven by witnesses or pregnancy or confession." Sufyan added, "I have memorized this narration in this way." Umar added, "Surely Allah's Apostle carried out the penalty of Rajam, and so did we after him" (8:536–37; 82.16.816).

Surah 4:15–16 states that those guilty of fornication are to "be confined to their houses until death take them." Surah 24:2 changes the penalty for sexual promiscuity: "The adulterer and the adulteress scourge ye each one of them with a hundred stripes. And let not pity for the twain withhold you from obedience to Allah."

Not one word in the Quran indicates sexual sins are to be punished by stoning the guilty parties. But Muhammad and his disciples are reported to have enforced this extreme penalty. Today in certain Muslim countries stoning is carried out in public. To me, it is clear such actions are extra-Quranic and cannot be sustained by reference to the highest source of Islamic authority. At this point the Hadith comes into direct conflict with the Quran. It appears that some fundamentalist Muslim authorities have chosen to heed the Hadith rather than the Quran.

These various conflicts are largely ignored (or unknown) by most Muslims. It would seem appropriate for Muslims to be asked to focus on these issues in their public debates with Christians rather than attacking doctrines of the Trinity and biblical authority.

Muslims and Quranic Application

The sons of Ishmael have always revered the Quran. A person who disciplines himself to memorize the total revelation, which is approximately the size of the New Testament, is known as a

Hafiz. The Hadith extols Muslims who are among the select few who have accomplished such a worthy task.

> Narrated Aisha: The Prophet said, "Such a person as recites the Quran and masters it by heart, will be with the noble righteous scribes (in Heaven). And such a person as exerts himself to learn the Quran by heart, and recites it with great difficulty, will have a double reward" (6:431–32; 60.332.459).

Receiving the blessing of Allah is important to the devout Muslim. A vehicle of transmission of God's favor is combining the quoting of the Quran with rubbing one's hands over the entire body. This act is a physical application of Allah's Word in a sense of blessing and protection.

> Narrated Aisha: Whenever the Prophet went to bed every night, he used to cup his hands together and blow over it after reciting Surat Al-Ikhlas, Surat Al-Falaq and Surat An-Nas, and then rub his hands over whatever parts of his body he was able to rub, starting with his head, face and front of his body. He used to do that three times (6:495; 61.14.536).

From the earliest days of Muslim history, emotion has had an integral part in binding together the community of the faithful. Part of this may be due to the Arab personality, but I have found Muslims worldwide to be prone to religious feelings that are resident deep in the psyche. This is often revealed in expressed emotions of joy, tears, or even anger if Islam is in any sense threatened. One such illustration of emotional outbursts took place in the life of Abu Bakr.

> Narrated Aisha: My father Abu Bakr thought of building a mosque in the courtyard of his house and he did so. He used to pray and recite the Quran in it. The pagan women and their children used to stand by him and look at him with surprise. Abu Bakr was a soft-hearted person and could not help weeping while reciting the Quran. The chiefs of the Quraish pagans became afraid of that (i.e. that their children and women might be affected by the recitation of Quran) (1:276; 8.86.465).

The initial recorders of Quranic revelation regarded themselves as privileged persons. One such scribe was overwhelmed at the thought of God actually articulating his name.

> Narrated Anas bin Malik: Allah's Prophet said to Ubai bin Ka'b, "Allah has ordered me to recite the Quran to you." Ubai said, "Did Allah mention me by name to you?" The Prophet said, "Yes," Ubai said, "Have I been mentioned by the Lord of the World?" The Prophet said, "Yes." Then Ubai burst into tears (6:457; 60.349.485).

Muhammad's wife Aisha was once accused of immorality with a young soldier. This was a most serious charge for Aisha, the Prophet, and the emerging Islamic community who were watching closely to see how Muhammad would handle this accusation. It was resolved through a special Quranic revelation directly from Allah. Variant but substantially similar accounts of this happening are repeated numerous times throughout the Hadith (see also chap. 17).

> Narrated Aisha: By Allah I never thought that Allah would reveal Divine Inspiration in my case, as I considered myself too inferior to be talked of in the Holy Quran. I had hoped that Allah's Apostle might have a dream in which Allah would prove my innocence. By Allah, Allah's Apostle had not got up and nobody had left the house before the Divine Inspiration came to Allah's Apostle. So there overtook him the same state which used to overtake him, (which he used to have on being inspired divinely). He was sweating so much so that the drops of the sweat were dropping like pearls though it was a (cold) wintery day. When that state of Allah's Apostle was over, he was smiling and the first word he said was "Aisha! Thank Allah, for Allah has declared your innocence." My mother told me to go to Allah's Apostle. I replied, "By Allah, I will not go to him and will not thank but Allah" So Allah revealed: *"Verily! They who spread the slander are a gang among you. . . ."* (Quran 24:11) (3:510–11; 48.15.829).

In my sojourn among Muslims, I have noted women are extremely careful to go into a bathroom only when they are not being observed by nonfamily members. Perhaps some of this reluctance stems from an incident in the life of a wife of the Prophet.

Narrated Aisha: Sauda (the wife of the Prophet) went out to answer the call of nature after it was made obligatory (for all the Muslim ladies) to observe the veil. She was a fat huge lady, and everybody who knew her before could recognize her. So Umar bin Al-Khat-tab saw her and said, "O Sauda! By Allah, you cannot hide yourself from us, so think of a way to which you should not be recognized on going out. Sauda returned while Allah's Apostle was in my house taking his supper and a bone covered with meat was in his hand. She entered and said, "O Allah's Apostle! I went out to answer the call of nature and Umar said to me so-and-so." Then Allah inspired him (the Prophet) and when the bone was still in his hand as he had not put it down, he said (to Sauda), "You (women) have been allowed to go out for your needs" (6:300–301; 60.241.318).

It is interesting that Allah gave a revelation on such a mundane subject. One can only ponder what alternatives could have been utilized in a culture where excretory functions were generally performed behind the nearest sand dune.

We are indebted to the Hadith for opening a window on the historical background of the Quran. Pondering the process of the compilation and application of the central Scriptures of the Islamic faith helps us to move one step closer to truly understanding the world's second-largest religion. It is not appropriate to use this material to aggressively attack the Quran's inadequacies. But, upon establishing a positive relationship with a Muslim, one can enter into a careful dialogue on the systems of scriptural inspiration as claimed by Islam and Christianity respectively. I find it difficult to be passive as Muslims make outlandish statements undermining the integrity of biblical authority. Seldom are they aware of their own problems. But, be aware, this is a most sensitive subject. Muslims are ready to attack but not to be attacked. Salman Rushdie will readily attest to this fact.

2

Salvation

e can say simplistically that Islam teaches that eternal life is obtained by faith in Allah and by performance of good deeds. The cognitive affirmation, "There is no deity apart from Allah, and Muhammad is his Prophet," is the primary entrée into the worldwide community of Islam. This verbalization of faith is to be accompanied by works compatible with the teaching of the Quran and Hadith.

Muslims believe there is no spiritual salvation for devotees of false religions. Islam teaches an emphatic "One Way" to knowing God. The only exception is for those who have never heard of the Islamic plan of salvation. God will be merciful to such people.

Christians and Jews are said to have been turned away from the true faith:

> Narrated Abu Huraira: Allah's Apostle said: "No child is born but has the Islamic Faith, but its parents turn it into a Jew or a Christian" (8:389–90; 77.2.597).

So, in a sense, all Christians and Jews have been apostatized by their parents. I have found this belief to be common among Muslims. This religious understanding can lead to a measure of arrogance on the part of Muslims who feel that Christianity and Judaism are aberrant Islam.

The Hadith complements the Quran by supplying details and additions to Islamic soteriology, which will be explored topically as sin, faith, and good deeds.

Sin

> Narrated Al-Harith bin Suwaid: The Prophet said: "A believer sees his sins as if he were sitting under a mountain which, he is afraid, may fall on him; whereas the wicked person considers his sins as flies passing over his nose and he just drives them away" (8:214;75.4.320).

This verse certainly presents an ideal, but it may be far from reality. Indeed, I have known Muslims fearful of the impact of sin in their lives. One attorney who is also a teacher of the Quran related that his concern about sexual lust leads him to fast every Friday in an effort to obtain mental purity. On the other hand, most Muslims I have met are quite passive over the impact sin may have in their everyday existence.

Muhammad defined two focuses of transgression.

> Narrated Sahl bin Sad: Narrated Allah's Apostle: "Whoever can guarantee (the chastity of) what is between his two jaw-bones and what is between his two legs (i.e. his tongue and his private parts), I guarantee Paradise for him" (8:320; 76.23.481).

Wayward speech and illicit sex, then, draw the Muslim away from the path of Allah. Muhammad, however, distinguished thoughts and action:

> Narrated Abu Huraira: The Prophet said, "Allah has forgiven my followers the evil thoughts that occur in their minds, as long as such thoughts are not put into action or uttered" (7:147; 63.11.194).

It is to be noted that sinful thoughts, though not as corrupting as evil deeds, still need to be forgiven. One should bear in mind that at the time Muhammad shared these ideas he, claiming Allah's sanction, possessed at least nine wives. His followers were allowed four spouses each. Perhaps it would be legitimate to ask why evil thoughts would be a problem in light of having such a multiplicity of sexual partners. My Muslim friend has three wives, the most recent acquisition being thirty years his junior! He has also divorced three other wives.

Another sin highlighted in the Hadith is greed.

> Narrated Sahl bin Sad: The Prophet said: "If the son of Adam were given a valley full of gold, he would love to have a second one; and if he were given the second one, he would love to have a third, for nothing fills the belly of Adam's son except dust [death]" (8:297; 76.10.446).

On a practical level, I would say sex is more a moral aberration among Muslims than is greed. Or it may be that the deprived economic status of most inhabitants of the Islamic Two-Thirds World causes the compulsion for material goods to be on an elementary level, such as the desire to own a watch. Thus, it is not blatant in its outworking and consequently not noticeable as significant to a Western observer.

There continues to be controversy on the subject of whether the Prophet was a sinner. Some Muslim theologians deny and others affirm such a possibility. Middle-ground advocates favor the position that says Muhammad sinned prior to his apostolic calling but subsequently was kept by Allah in moral and ethical purity, a view that seems to be contradicted in a Hadith transmitted by Aisha.

> Narrated Aisha: I heard the Prophet and listened to him before his death while he was lying supported on his back, and he was saying, "O Allah! Forgive me, and bestow Your Mercy on me, and let me meet the highest" (5:511; 59.81.715).

The Quran also has several references to the Prophet repenting from sin. It would appear his salvation was dependent on faith, good deeds, repentance of sin, requesting the forgiveness of God, and finally, the mercy of Allah . . . a formula for obtaining salvation followed by Muslims down through the centuries.

Faith

Islam places great priority on faith. But faith can be a prism of many ideological and religious complexions. It can also be adjunct to or absolutely central to life. Muhammad set the direction by declaring the Allah of Islam to be the fount of all truth.

You are the Truth, and Your Word is the Truth (9:359; 93.8.483).

Without a firm and unshakable faith in the God of truth and in his word, the Quran, there can be no salvation for the Muslim. In fact, as this Hadith points out, faith is even more important than the performance of good works.

Narrated Abu Dhar: Allah's Apostle said: "The Angel Gabriel came and said to me, 'Whoever amongst your followers dies, worshipping none along with Allah, will enter Paradise.' I said, 'Even if he did such-and-such things (i.e. even if he stole or committed illegal sexual intercourse).' He said, 'Yes.'" (3:337; 41.3.573).

The importance of loving Allah is also highlighted.

Narrated Anas bin Malik: While the Prophet and I were coming out of the mosque, a man met us outside the gate. The man said, "O Allah's Apostle! When will be the Hour?" The Prophet asked him, "What have you prepared for it?" The man became afraid and ashamed and then said, "O Allah's Apostle! I haven't prepared for it with fasts, prayers or charitable gifts but I love Allah and His Apostle." The Prophet said, "You will be with the one whom you love" (9:199; 89.10.267).

Repetition of Quranic creedal statements strengthens the Muslim's faith in Allah. One can question whether this leads to a type of brainwashing. Consider this exhortation to engage in a recitation one hundred times each day.

Narrated Abu Huraira: The Prophet said: "If one says one hundred times in one day: 'No one has the right to be worshipped but Allah, and he Alone Who has no partners, to Him belongs Dominion and to Him belong all the Praises, and He has power over all things (i.e. Omnipotent),' one will get the reward of manumitting [freeing] ten slaves, and one hundred good deeds will be written in his account, and one hundred bad deeds will be wiped off or erased from his account, and on that day he will be protected from the morning till evening from Satan, and nobody will be superior to him except one who has done more than that which he has done" (4:327; 54.10.514).

A similar Hadith states,

> Narrated Abu Huraira: Allah's Apostle said, "Whoever says, 'Subhan Allah wa bihamdihi' (I deem Allah free of any resemblance to anything what-so-ever in any respect, and I celebrate His Praises) one hundred times a day, will be forgiven all his sins even if they were as much as the foam of the Sea" (8:277; 75.67.414).

Here we see a theological statement of faith is integrated into the process of God's forgiving sin. For each recitation one good deed is added to the believer's account with God and at the same time one bad deed is deleted. I have read of Muslims repeating Quranic verses thousands of times in order to become more assured of their eternal salvation.

The focus of these recitations often centers on the absolute unity of God. "Allah has no partners" and "has no resemblance to anything whatsoever in any respect" are both slanted toward a denial of the Christian view of Father, Son, and Holy Spirit as all being uniquely and mysteriously God. No wonder Muslims react so vociferously against the doctrine of the Trinity when they are unwaveringly committed to a theological position that directly attacks this biblical truth.

Reinforcing this observation is the following recorded opinion of Muhammad:

> Narrated Abu Said: A man heard another man reciting:
>
> *"Say (O Muhammad): 'He is Allah, the One.'"* (Quran 112:1)
>
> And he recited it repeatedly. When it was morning, he went to the Prophet and informed him about that as if he considered that the recitation of the Surah by itself was not enough. Allah's Apostle said, "By Him in Whose Hand my life is, it is equal to one-third of the Quran" (9:349–50; 93.1.471).

Real, vital faith, according to Muslim theologians, must lead on to a grid of works as prescribed by the Quran and Hadith.

Good Deeds

Despite the Muslim's penchant for a strong, even absolute, belief in the sovereignty of God, he still unequivocally affirms the necessity of his own contribution to the salvific process.

> Narrated Ali: While the Prophet was in a funeral procession, he picked up something and started scraping the ground with it, and said, "There is none among you but has his place assigned for him either in Hell Fire or in Paradise." They said, "O Allah's Apostle! Shall we not depend upon what has been written for us and give up deeds?" He said, "Carry on doing (good) deeds . . ." (6:446; 60.343.474).

Muhammad, in the Hadith or elsewhere, does not delve into the philosophical or theological nuances of this controversy. He prefers to let both teachings stand on their own merit.

Illustrations abound in the Traditions of what actually constitutes good deeds. One of the more colorful stories comes from the lips of Muhammad himself.

> Narrated Ibn Umar: The Prophet said: "While three persons were walking, rain began to fall and they had to enter a cave in a mountain. A big rock rolled over and blocked the mouth of the cave. They said to each other, 'Invoke Allah with the best deed you have performed (so Allah might remove the rock).' One of them said, 'O Allah! My parents were old and I used to go out for grazing (my animals). On my return I would milk (the animals) and take the milk in a vessel to my parents to drink. After they had drunk from it, I would give it to my children, family and wife. One day I was delayed and on my return I found my parents sleeping, and I disliked to wake them up. The children were crying at my feet (because of hunger). That state of affairs continued till it was dawn. O Allah! If You regard that I did it for Your sake, then please remove this rock so that we may see the sky.' So, the rock was moved a bit. The second said, 'O Allah! You know that I was in love with a cousin of mine, like the deepest love a man may have for a woman, and she told me that I would not get my desire fulfilled unless I paid her one hundred Dinars (gold pieces). So, I struggled for it till I

gathered the desired amount, and when I sat in between her legs, she told me to be afraid of Allah, and asked me not to deflower her except rightfully (by marriage). So, I got up and left her. O Allah! If You regard that I did it for Your sake, kindly remove this rock.' So, two-thirds of the rock was removed. Then the third man said, 'O Allah! No doubt You know that once I employed a worker for one Faraq (three Sa's) of millet, and when I wanted to pay him, he refused to take it, so I sowed it and from its yield I bought cows and a shepherd. After a time that man came and demanded his money. I said to him: Go to those cows and the shepherd and take them for they are for you. He asked me whether I was joking with him. I told him that I was not joking with him, and all that belonged to him. O Allah! If You regard that I did it sincerely for Your sake, then please remove the rock.' So, the rock was removed completely from the mouth of the cave" (3:228–29; 34.100.418).

Feeding and caring for aged parents and young children; avoiding fornication; and treating one's employee fairly all qualify as works that please Allah and bring about his divine intervention in moving the rock. When one reads such highly regarded Islamic literature, there emerges an understanding of the Muslim hierarchy of what is pleasing and displeasing to God. Reward from God as an incentive to holy living is a basic teaching of the story.

A number of Hadith unequivocally link one's actions to his eternal abode.

Narrated Abu Huraira: Allah's Apostle said: "All my followers will enter Paradise except those who refuse." They said, "O Allah's Apostle! Who will refuse?" He said, "Whoever obeys me will enter Paradise, and whoever disobeys me is the one who refuses (to enter it)" (9:284; 92.2.384).

Here we see the preeminent position of Muhammad in Islam. The Prophet has not commanded his followers to obey Allah upon threat of exclusion from paradise. He has clearly stated that obedience to himself is the focus and criterion for one's entry into heaven. This is a rather awesome statement. The Muslim response to our incredulity is to affirm that Muhammad's life and teaching were so attuned to Allah that his commands were only a reflection of the will of God. Therefore, Muhammad, like the apostle Paul, could say to his audience, "Follow me."

The community of believers is always a central focus in Islam. To onlooking witnesses one is accountable for one's deeds and character; even eternal destiny is entrusted to these witnesses:

> Narrated Abu Al-Aswad: The Apostle said, "Allah will admit into Paradise any Muslim whose good character is attested by four persons." We asked the Prophet, "If there were three witnesses only?" He said, "Even three." We asked, "If there were two only?" He said, "Even two." But we did not ask him about one witness (3:492; 48.6.811).

Good deeds and forgiveness of sin are inextricably woven together in Islamic teaching.

> Narrated Abu Said Al-Khudri: Allah's Apostle said: "If a person embraces Islam sincerely, then Allah shall forgive all his past sins, and after that starts the settlements of accounts: the reward of his good deeds will be ten times to seven hundred times for each good deed" (1:36; 2.32.39).

From the beginning of Islamic history there have been conversions that have emanated from less than ethical and moral considerations. In contemporary times, I have noted this in one Asian country. A significant number of Roman Catholic contract workers seeking employment in the Middle East have made a shallow profession of faith in Islam in order to facilitate job opportunities. It appears that local Muslim leaders have done nothing to inhibit this practice. Perhaps they trust to move such a nominal conversion to one of greater depth and reality.

This Hadith specifies that a person will receive forgiveness of sins only if he or she has demonstrated sincerity in embracing Islam. But this is only the beginning of the settlement of accounts. Good and bad deeds are in constant tension. This Hadith presents a strange range of rewards. It seems good works will be multiplied many times on the great judgment day. In Bangladesh, large segments of Muslims attribute multiplied thousands of merit points to each act of prayer *(salat)* that is performed.

Lest the non-Muslim reader overemphasize the works aspect of Islamic teaching regarding salvation, there is a definite focus on the mercy of Allah.

Narrated Abu Huraira: Allah's Apostle said: "The deeds of anyone of you will not save you (from the (Hell) Fire)." They said,
"Even you (will not be saved by your deeds). O Allah's Apostle?"
He said, "No, even I (will not be saved) unless and until Allah
bestows His Mercy on me. Therefore, do good deeds properly, sincerely and moderately, and worship Allah in the forenoon and in
the afternoon and during a part of the night, and always adopt a
middle, moderate, regular course whereby you will reach your target (Paradise)" (8:313; 76.18.470).

This is the concluding word on Islam and eternal salvation.
Faith and works are evident dynamics. But without the unde-
served mercy of God, there can be no hope of paradise for the
community of the faithful.

Christians can feel free to interchange the words *grace* and
mercy as we witness to Muslims. God's mercy, to the believer in
biblical revelation, has Christ as the focus of the divine plan of
salvation. We have a concrete and definitive systemization of
God's initiative and man's desired response. Islam, on the other
hand, leans largely toward the subjective. How many prayers or
good works guarantee eternal salvation? The answer is uncer-
tain. This causes Muslims to be unsure concerning any degree of
salvific assurance.

This distinction between Islam and Christianity provides a definite opportunity for witness. Through a focus on the substitu-
tionary work of Christ on the cross for all of the human race, one
is invited to direct one's faith and allegiance to the great Source
of eternal salvation.

Islam recognizes the "threat of the cross" and has undercut its
message by saying Christ did not die on the tree, but rather
ascended directly to heaven. This denial is one of the great bar-
riers to Muslims' coming to the Lord. We pray for enlightenment
among the children of Ishmael in this crucial area.

uhammad

ew men in the world have so affected the human race historically and contemporarily as has the Prophet of the desert. To Muslims, Muhammad's words and deeds are as fresh, vital, and binding in the present as they were when first spoken more than thirteen hundred years ago. At times, it seems as though Muhammad is almost deified by his followers.

Conversely, this apostle of the ages is cursed, maligned, and contradicted by multiplied thousands. His legacy is declared to engender hatred and violence. Christians tend to make direct comparisons between Jesus, who is presented in the Bible as without sin, and Muhammad, whom they hold personally responsible for all the sins of modern-day Muslims. Seldom in history has there been such long-standing and deep antagonism between two religious systems as that which we see outworking today within Christian-Muslim relationships.

Muhammad is the point man. What do we do with him? Is it possible to strip him of myth and romantic legend? Can we trace and authoritatively identify the historical Muhammad? Many have tried. Thousands of books have been written about the messenger of Allah. However, it is my considered opinion that the academic approach to unveiling the real Muhammad results in an admixture of truth and fiction.

What really affects the world today is a Muhammad shrouded in a mystical fog. The ethereal presence of Muhammad hovers over Islam and powerfully elicits a dynamic, emotional response. A Bangladeshi poet maligns the Prophet and is thrown into prison. In the Philippines a Christian young man openly denigrates Muhammad before an audience of Muslims. Soon thereafter, a grenade is thrown into the midst of a public meeting sponsored by the man's organization. Two young women are killed and thirty-eight other Christians are injured. One dares to criticize Muhammad only at the risk of personal harm.

Though a Hadith-centered study of Muhammad has inbuilt inadequacies, it is still probably the best and most authoritative insight into the words and actions of the Prophet. This chapter highlights a selection of descriptions of Muhammad as he lived and functioned in the seventh century.

Physique

One writer offers this all-embracive evaluation of Muhammad:

Narrated Anas: Allah's Apostle was the (most handsome), most generous and the bravest of all the people (4:173; 52.165.277).

Ethnocentrism is evident in the phrase *of all the people.* There is little doubt that the writer's knowledge and travel were limited to but a few thousand people in a small area of Arabia.

An interesting Tradition alludes to Muhammad's seal of prophethood:

Narrated As-Saib bin Yazid: I stood behind him and saw the seal of Prophethood between his shoulders, and it was like the "Zir-al-Hijlah" (means the button of a small tent, but some said 'egg of a partridge') (1:130; 4.42.189).

This is the only Hadith I am aware of that mentions such a seal. No Muslim has ever alluded to it in my presence. It would seem that the reference is so vague as to prohibit any authoritative exposition of the phenomenon.

The Traditions also give a more general description:

Narrated Rabi'a Abdur-Rahman: I heard Anas bin Malik describing the Prophet saying, "He was a medium height amongst the people, neither tall nor short; he had a rose colour, neither absolutely white nor deep brown; his hair was neither completely curly nor quite lank. . . . When he expired, he had scarcely twenty white hairs in his head and beard." Rabi'a said, "I saw some of his hair and it was red. When I asked about that, I was told that it turned red because of scent" (4:487; 56.22.747).

Many devout Muslims dye their hair and/or beard a rather dull red. This Hadith may be the point of reference for this practice. Two commentators observed:

Narrated Abdullah bin Abbas: The Prophet used to keep his hair falling loose . . . (5:193; 58.50.280).

Narrated Malik: The hair of the Prophet used to hang near his shoulders (7:520; 72.68.788).

In Western society, body odors are to be disguised and neutralized by mouth fresheners, colognes, and deodorants. Throughout much of the Islamic world such smells are not considered offensive. Part of the reason is simply economic: cosmetics are costly. However, several Traditions refer to Muhammad's sweat in a positive manner. Therefore his followers hold a similar view about their own bodies.

Narrated Anas: I have never touched silk or *Dibaj* (i.e. thick silk) softer than the palm of the Prophet, nor have I smelt a perfume nicer than the sweat of the Prophet (4:492; 56.22.761).

Narrated Abu Juhaifa: After the prayer, the people got up and held the hands of the Prophet and passed them on their faces. I also took his hand and kept it on my face and noticed that it was colder than ice, and its smell was nicer than musk (4:489; 56.22.753).

Was the Prophet a morose melancholic or a bubbly sanguine? Muhammad's temperament is inferred from a number of indirect references. Like most of the human race, he seemed to have his moments of elation as well as periods of depression. Muhammad

was certainly an intense person. A representative Hadith highlights his physical expression of happiness.

> Narrated Abdullah Malik: Whenever Allah's Apostle became
> happy, his face would shine as if it were a piece of moon, and we
> all knew that characteristic of him (5:503; 59.78.702).

More important than Muhammad's physical features, however, is his character.

Character

Muhammad was initially overwhelmed when the revelations
from Allah commenced. There were moments when he doubted
his sanity. The Prophet's faithful wife, Khadija, became concerned
and took him to Waraqa, her Christian cousin. A pivotal moment
in Islamic history occurred as this Arab believer in Christ affirmed
Muhammad's communication as being from God.

> Narrated Aisha: Khadija then accompanied [Muhammad] to her
> cousin Waraqa who, during the Pre-Islamic Period became a Chris-
> tian and used to write with Hebrew letters. He would write from
> the gospel in Hebrew as much as Allah wished him to write. He
> was an old man and had lost his eyesight. Khadija said to Waraqa,
> "Listen to the story of your nephew, O my cousin!" Waraqa asked,
> "O my nephew! What have you seen?" Allah's Apostle described
> whatever he had seen. Waraqa said, "This is the same one who
> keeps the secrets (angel Gabriel) whom Allah had sent to Moses.
> I wish I were young and could live to the time when your people
> would turn you out." Allah's Apostle asked, "Will they drive me
> out?" Waraqa replied in the affirmative and said, "Anyone who
> came with something similar to what you have brought was treated
> with hostility; and if I should remain alive till the day when you
> will be turned out then I would support you strongly." But after a
> few days Waraqa died and the Divine Inspiration was also paused
> for a while (1:4; 1.1.3).

It would appear that Muhammad received courage to press on
from this prophetical word of Waraqa. Along with this timely
confirmation came the startling announcement that persecution
would soon follow. Nonetheless Muhammad did not flinch from

that which he considered to be his calling from Allah. Muslim theologians point to hostility and suffering as forces that helped form the tenacious character of the Prophet.

In earlier times the Prophet's suffering sprang from persecution; as he aged, his suffering was physical. Aisha was in a position to closely observe his struggles with a weakened body.

> Narrated Aisha: I never saw anybody suffering so much from a sickness as Allah's Apostle (7:373; 70.2.549).

Throughout history, rulers of all descriptions have tended to adopt an ostentatious style of life. Unfortunately, religious leaders have not been spared this temptation to enjoy the trappings of power. Muslims are quick to point out that their religious model retained a godly character.

> Narrated Ibn Abbas: Allah's Apostle smiled while he was lying on a mat made of palm tree leaves with nothing between him and the mat. Underneath his head there was a leather pillow stuffed with palm fibres, and leaves of a saut tree were piled at his feet, and above his head hung a few waterskins. On seeing the marks of the mat imprinted on his side, I wept. He said, 'Why are you weeping?' I replied, 'O Allah's Apostle! Caesar and Khosrau are leading the luxurious life while you, Allah's Apostle are living in destitution.' The Prophet then replied, 'Won't you be satisfied that they enjoy this world and we the Hereafter?' (6:408; 60.316.435).

A rejoinder to this position may include the fact that Muhammad had at least nine wives at one time. Minimally, this involved a separate room for every spouse, plus supplying the usual needs each wife would have. This would not seem to indicate voluntary or excessive poverty. Issues like this are seldom noted by Muslim expositors; indeed, two Traditions highlight that the Prophet did have some measure of wealth at his demise:

> Narrated Amir bin Al-Harith: Allah's Apostle did not leave a Dinar or a Dirham or a male or a female slave. He left only his white mule on which he used to ride, and his weapons, and a piece of land which he gave in charity for the needy travellers (5:526; 59.8.738).

Narrated Abu Huraira: Allah's Apostle said: "Not even a single Dinar of my property should be distributed (after my death) to my inheritors, but whatever I leave excluding the provisions for my wives and my servants, should be spent in charity" (8:475; 80.3.721).

Humility is a virtue appreciated by most of mankind. Almost always, religions promote their founder as a humble person. Islam is no exception.

Narrated Umar: The Prophet stated, "Do not exaggerate in praising me as the Christians praised the son of Mary, for I am only a Slave. So, call me the Slave of Allah and His Apostle" (4:435; 55.43.654).

Unfortunately, Muhammad misunderstood the Christian practice as unduly exalting a mere man. Never in the Quran or the Al-Bukhari Hadith do we see Jesus presented as divine. Conversely, Christ is consistently set forth as a prophet without claim to deity. Therefore, Muhammad felt justified in criticizing the followers of Christ for engaging in a type of idolatry. Muhammad, by contrast, referred to himself as a slave. This was done in a culture in which slaves were commonly found and such a reference was well understood.

An indication of the Prophet's sensitivity to others is found in this Hadith:

Narrated Ibn Masud: The Prophet used to take care of us in preaching by selecting a suitable time, so that we might not get bored. (He abstained from pestering us with sermons and knowledge all the time) (1:60; 3.12.68).

Various images of Muhammad have been presented by non-Muslim historians and Islamists. These portraits tend toward presenting an arrogant, sensual, and militaristic leader. In contrast to their profile is this Tradition.

Narrated Abu Sa'id Al-Khudri: The Prophet was shier than a veiled virgin girl (4:492; 56.22.762).

Muslims have considered their Prophet to have had an impeccable character. They continue to look to the Hadith for authentication of their claim.

Negative Characteristics of Muhammad

At the outset it should be noted that definitions of character imperfections will vary from culture to culture. Lying, stealing, and fornication, to name but a few sins that are fairly well defined in the West, will not be so clearly labeled as transgressions among certain peoples. (Even within a culture the definitions may vary; a number of states have laws against adultery by consenting adults, but many Americans scoff at such "obsolete" legislation.)

As we look at the life of Muhammad we are confronted with a clash of perspective. What I present next from the Hadith will not be regarded by Muslims as sin in the life of the Prophet. They will interpret it as a contextual problem, a historical variation, or an obscurity yet to be resolved. So it is with an acknowledgment of my cultural and theological bias that I set forth the following Traditions accompanied by my interpretative comments.

Some Hadith indicate Muhammad had a healthy self-image. To many students of Islam, these citations seem to point to an overactive ego. Muslims would say these statements of Muhammad only set forth the facts.

Narrated Jabir bin Abdullah: The Prophet said, "I have been given five things which were not given to any one else before me.

1. Allah made me victorious by awe, (by His frightening my enemies) for a distance of one month's journey.
2. The earth has been made for me (and for my followers) a place for praying and a thing to perform Tayammum, therefore anyone of my followers can pray wherever the time of a prayer is due.
3. The booty has been made Halal (lawful) for me yet it was not lawful for anyone else before me.
4. I have been given the right of intercession (on the Day of Resurrection).
5. Every Prophet used to be sent to his nation only but I have been sent to all mankind" (1:199–200; 7.1.331).

A careful reading of these five declarations helps me to understand the absolute dogmatism of most Muslims worldwide. They cannot countenance the thought that they might be wrong or that another religion may have claim to universal truth. Recently, I was talking to an intelligent and dedicated follower of the Prophet. I sought to convince him of the need to compare the conflicting claims of Islam and Christianity. He, politely but with emphasis, told me there is absolutely no need to investigate Christianity. Truth, he said, is in Islam; reading counterclaims may just be used of Satan to bring about cognitive confusion. But, before we become too critical, would not many Christians respond in a similar manner if a Muslim sought to persuade them to seriously consider Islam as a viable alternative to their faith in Christ?

Apart from the issue of truth, we still observe Muhammad's projecting himself in a unique manner. He states that his enemies hold him in awe; the earth has been made for him; he alone has the right to intercede for Muslims on judgment day; and he, unlike other prophets (including Jesus), has been sent as a messenger of Allah to all the human race. That is quite a menu of distinctions.

Another Hadith has Muhammad urging his followers to love him supremely.

> Narrated Anas: The Prophet said: "None of you will have faith till he loves me more than his faith, his children and all mankind" (1:20; 2.8.14).

More people throughout the world have the name *Muhammad* than any other name. This phenomenon did not occur accidentally. The Prophet commanded the practice.

> Narrated Abu Huraira: The Prophet said, "Name yourselves after me . . . and whoever sees me in a dream, he surely sees me, for Satan cannot impersonate me. And whoever intentionally ascribes something to me falsely, he will surely take his place in the (Hell) Fire" (8:139–40; 72.109.217).

Is it not an extreme position for Muhammad to sentence someone to hell for a verbal sin?

Another example of the Prophet's self-exaltation is his declaration that he will be chief among all people in paradise.

Narrated Abu Huraira: We were in the company of the Prophet at a banquet and a cooked (mutton) forearm was set before him, and he used to like it. He ate a morsel of it and said, "I will be the chief (i.e. best) of all the people on the Day of Resurrection" (4:350; 55.3.556).

Muhammad lived in an age of warfare. In large measure it was a day of the "survival of the fittest." Thus, the Prophet evidently desired to make a show of his physical strength.

Narrated Ibn Abbas: The Prophet hastened in going around the Ka'ba and between the Safa and Marwa in order to show the pagans his strength (5:391; 59.42.558).

This seems a stark contrast to Christ and the cross. Jesus could have called for divine intervention but instead opted for ignominious suffering and death.

Anger was not unknown to the Prophet.

Narrated Aisha: The Prophet entered while there was a curtain having pictures (of animals) in the house. His face got red with anger, and then he got hold of the curtain and tore it into pieces. The Prophet said, "Such people as paint these pictures will receive the severest punishment on the Day of Resurrection" (8:83–84; 72.75.130).

This Hadith is widely known among Muslims, and the more orthodox resolutely refuse to have any pictures in their homes. Some confine the prohibition to depictions of animals; others extend it to include even photos of family members. Shiite Muslims generally disregard such strictures and even allow pictorial representations of Muhammad. This practice is strictly prohibited among Sunnis. I well recall watching a large and boisterous procession making its way past our village home in Bangladesh. The participants' anger was being directed toward an American publication that had the audacity to reproduce a painting of Muhammad. These Muslims would justify their wrath as being allied with the anger of their Prophet.

It is possible that Muhammad, living as he did in an idolatrous society, was expressing concern over the danger that his followers would worship pictorial representations. This concern, however, is not stated.

It would appear that the Prophet had killed persons:

> Narrated Abu Qilaba: . . . Allah's Apostle never killed anyone except in one of the following three situations: (1) A person who killed somebody unjustly, was killed (in Qisas) (2) a married person who committed illegal sexual intercourse and (3) a man who fought against Allah and His Apostle and deserted Islam and became an apostate (9:26; 83.22.37).

From this and other Traditions comes the authorization to execute adulterers. The law of apostasy is also well defined in this passage (this will be discussed further in chapter 9).

The Demise of Muhammad

Prior to his death the Prophet expressed a number of concerns:

> Narrated Anas bin Malik: Allah's Prophet said, "O Allah! I seek refuge with You from incapacity and laziness, from cowardice and geriatric old age, and seek refuge with You from the punishment of the grave, and I seek refuge with You from the afflictions of life and death" (8:252; 75.39.378).

Like most of us who are aging, the Prophet was concerned for his health. Interestingly, he also sought Allah's protection from laziness and cowardice. There is no indication he succumbed to these fleshly temptations.

In a Hadith filled with biblical parallels, we see Muhammad focusing on his eternal state as he approached death.

> Narrated Aisha: The Prophet said, "O Allah! Wash away my sins with the water of snow and hail, and cleanse my heart from sins as a white garment is cleansed of filth, and let there be a far distance between me and my sins as You have set far away the East and the West from each other" (8:257; 75.45.386).

Yet more amazing is another statement:

Narrated Abu Huraira: I heard Allah's Apostle saying, "By Allah! I ask for Allah's forgiveness and turn to Him in repentance more than seventy times a day" (8:213; 75.3.319).

And another Hadith suggests he was compulsive about asking for God's forgiveness.

Narrated Um al-Ala: The Prophet said, "By Allah, though I am the Apostle of Allah, yet I do not know what Allah will do to me."

[Translator's Note: No doubt, the Prophet knew that he would go to Paradise but he felt that the knowledge of the unseen should be referred to Allah] (5:183; 58.45.266).

The note following the Hadith highlights a conflict between Muhammad's self-evaluation and that which was strongly affirmed by his followers. The Prophet humbly doubted his worthiness to enter heaven while his disciples expressed no doubt about where Muhammad would spend eternity.

During the Prophet's life he made clear his opinion of worship at the shrine of a deceased person.

Narrated Aisha: Um Salma and Um Habiba had been to Ethiopia, and both of them narrated the Church's beauty and the pictures it contained. The Prophet raised his head and said, "Those are the people who, whenever a pious man dies amongst them, make a place of worship at his grave and then they place those pictures on it. They are the worst creatures in the sight of Allah" (2:238; 23.69.425).

This denouncement contradicts the practice of shrine worship that I have observed all over the Muslim world. Thousands of followers of Islamic "saints" regularly visit their graves to pray or to ask them to intercede to Allah in some area of felt need. There is little protest from orthodox Muslims concerning this decidedly unorthodox practice.

Today, the Prophet's gravesite in Medina, Saudi Arabia, is an integral part of the annual *Hajj* ceremony. Muslims from all over the world go to the tomb of Muhammad to pray, to ask for his intercession, and to give respect to the "latest and greatest" of all the prophets. These practices are in opposition to this Hadith.

Aisha said, "The Prophet in his fatal illness said, 'Allah cursed the Jews and the Christians because they took the graves of their Prophets as places for praying.'" Aisha added, "Had it not been for that, the grave of the Prophet would have been made prominent but I am afraid it still might be taken as a place for praying" (2:232; 23.60.414).

Aisha's fears have been realized.

There was great trauma among the disciples of Muhammad as word of his death spread. This Tradition highlights both the hesitation to accept the Prophet's demise as well as a challenge to follow only the living Allah.

> Narrated Aisha: The Prophet Allah's Apostle died while Abu Bakr was at a place called As-Sunah (Al-Aliya). Umar stood up and said, "By Allah! Allah's Apostle is not dead!" . . . Abu Bakr praised and glorified Allah and said, "No doubt! Whoever worshipped Muhammad, then Muhammad is dead, but whoever worshipped Allah, then Allah is alive and shall never die" (5:13; 57.6.19).

What do we make of the life and ministry of the Prophet? Are there bridges we can utilize between Muhammad and Christ?

Muhammad is presented as a dead sinner who is not to be worshiped. Christ is proclaimed biblically to be God-Man who is sinless and worthy of worship. The grave of Muhammad is in Medina. Christ's body ascended and is at the right hand of the Father.

We should avoid any type of attack on the character of the Prophet. Every reservation we may have will quickly be explained away by the devout Muslim. But the issues of Muhammad's humanness and ordinary death can be suggested to be in distinct contrast to Christ, who neither sinned nor remained in an earthly grave. Both of these facts are accepted by orthodox Muslims. I do not believe they give proper weight to these truths.

But, as history attests, these are extremely sensitive areas. Walk carefully and humbly!

iracles

*T*he Traditions are more concerned with the natural than with the supernatural. Life is worked out on the mundane level of everyday existence. An exception to this relates to a brief exposition of miracles scattered throughout the Hadith.

Multiplication of Food and Water

In several Hadith there are interesting parallels with Christ's multiplying the bread and fish for the five thousand and four thousand. A note accompanying this Tradition says that eighty poor people drank milk abundantly from one cup.

> Narrated Abu Huraira: They were admitted and took their seats in the house. The Prophet said, "O Aba Hirr!" I said, "Labbaik, O Allah's Apostle!" He said, "Take it and give it to them." So I took the bowl (of milk) and started giving it to one man who would drink his fill and return it to me, whereupon I would give it to another man who, in his turn, would drink his fill and return it to me, and I would then offer it to another man who would drink his fill and return it to me. Finally, after the whole group had drunk their fill, I reached the Prophet who took the bowl and put it on his hand, looked at me and smiled and said, "O Aba Hirr!" I replied, "Labbaik, O Allah's Apostle!" He said, "There remain you and I."

I said, "You have said the truth, O Allah's Apostle!" He said, "Sit down and drink." I sat down and drank. He said, "Drink," and I drank. He kept on telling me repeatedly to drink, till I said, "No, by Allah Who sent you with the Truth, I have no space for it (in my stomach)." He said, "Hand it over to me." When I gave him the bowl, he praised Allah and pronounced Allah's Name on it and drank the remaining milk (8:309; 76.17.459).

A further Hadith relates how a small amount of a meal greatly multiplied. There is no indication Muhammad is involved in this miracle.

Narrated Abdur Abi Bakr: By Allah, whenever we took a handful of the meal, the meal grew from underneath more than that handful until everybody ate to his satisfaction; yet the remaining food was more than the original meal. Abu Bakr saw that food was as much as or more than the original amount. He called his wife, "O sister of Bani Firas!" She said, "O pleasure of my eyes. The food has been tripled in quantity" (4:504; 56.24.781).

In another Hadith we see food multiplied through acts of Muhammad. One thousand people were able to eat abundantly from what was originally a small amount of food.

Narrated Jabir bin Abdullah: Then she brought out to him (i.e. the Prophet) the dough, and he spat in it and blessed it. Then he proceeded towards our earthenware meat-pot and spat in it and blessed it. Then he said (to my wife), "Call a lady-baker to bake along with you and keep on taking out scoops from your earthenware meat-pot, and do not put it down from its fireplace." They were one thousand (who took their meals), and by Allah they all ate, and then they left the food and went away. Our earthenware pot was still bubbling (full of meat) as if it had not decreased, and our dough was still being baked as if nothing had been taken from it (5:299; 59.28.428).

Water is a precious commodity in the desert. It is natural that a few of Muhammad's miracles would relate to quenching the thirst of his followers.

Narrated Al-Bara: We were one-thousand-and-four-hundred persons on the day of Al-Hudaibiya (Treaty), and Al-Hudaibiya was a well. We drew out its water not leaving even a single drop. The Prophet sat at the edge of the well and asked for some water with which he rinsed his mouth and then he threw it out into the well. We stayed for a short while and then drew water from the well and quenched our thirst, and even our riding animals drank water to their satisfaction (4:500; 56.24.777).

Twice in the Hadith we find accounts of water flowing from between Muhammad's fingers. In both instances there was a need, either to quench thirst or to provide water for prayer ablutions:

Narrated Abdullah: We used to consider miracles as Allah's Blessings, but you people consider them to be a warning. Once we were with Allah's Apostle on a journey, and we ran short of water. He said, "Bring the water remaining with you." The people brought a utensil containing a little water. He placed his hand in it and said, "Come to the blessed water, and the Blessing is from Allah." I saw the water flowing from among the fingers of Allah's Apostle, and no doubt, we heard the meal glorifying Allah, when it was being eaten (by him) (4:502; 56.24.779).

I'm not sure what noises a meal makes while glorifying Allah. Perhaps this refers to sounds Muhammad made while eating.

Narrated Thabit Anas: The Prophet asked for water and a tumbler with a broad base and not so deep, containing a small quantity of water, was brought to him whereby he put his fingers in it. Anas further said, "I noticed the water springing out from amongst his fingers." Anas added, "I estimated that the people who performed ablution with it numbered between seventy to eighty" (1:135; 4.48.199).

In all of my reading, I have never come across a supernatural act that exactly parallels these. It defies logical understanding that a great amount of water could gush forth from one's hand. But the Muslim handles it in the same way Christians assent to biblical miracles. Faith is the instrument to acceptance of the mysterious. Because of our presuppositions, we confidently affirm the inexplicable in our belief system while registering amazement that others could have "blind faith" in their miracles. Both sets of unexplainable phenomena are equally incredible to the onlooking secularist. This is not stated to undercut the validity of biblical miracles. Rather, I make the point to prod us toward a more balanced and sensitive evaluation of that which is held to be precious to those of the Islamic faith.

In another Hadith the Prophet is seen clearing the debts of a disciple through an act that combines a miracle with entrepreneurship.

> Narrated Jabir Al-Ansari: My father was martyred on the day of Uhud and left six daughters and some debts to be paid. When the time of plucking the fruits came, I went to Allah's Apostle and said, "O Allah's Apostle! You know that my father was martyred on Uhud's day and owed much debt, and I wish that the creditors would see you." The Prophet said, "Go and collect the various kinds of dates and place them separately in heaps." I did accordingly and called him. On seeing him, the creditors started claiming their rights pressingly at that time. When the Prophet saw how they behaved, he went round the biggest heap for three times and sat over it and said, "Call your companions (i.e. the creditors)." Then he kept on measuring and giving them, till Allah cleared all my father's debts. By Allah, it would have pleased me that Allah would clear the debts of my father even though I had not taken a single date to my sisters. But by Allah, all the heaps were complete, and I looked at the heap where Allah's Apostle was sitting and noticed it was as if not a single date had been taken (4:32–33; 51.37.40).

Other Miracles

Two incidents recorded in the Traditions defy the laws of nature. The first is the most famous because it is found in the Quran 54:1–3.

> *The hour drew nigh and the moon was rent in twain,*
> *And if they behold a portent they turn away and say:*
> *   Prolonged illusion.*
> *They denied (the Truth) and followed their own lusts.*

Some Muslim scholars prefer to regard this as an eschatological event. Their justification is to highlight the word *hour*. The "hour" of judgment will be a future day in which many strange and awesome things will occur, one of which will be the splitting of the moon.

Apart from the grammatical construction of the passage, which indicates a past happening, are the clear and unequivocal Traditions that elucidate this event in a historical context.

> Narrated Abdullah: The moon was cleft asunder while we were in the company of the Prophet, and it became two parts. The Prophet said, "Witness, witness (this miracle)" (6:365; 60.287.388).

Here Muhammad personally attests the reality of the split moon. A further Hadith seems to point to the Prophet actually causing the cleavage.

> Narrated Anas bin Malik: The people of Mecca asked Allah's Apostle to show them a miracle. So he showed the moon split in two halves between which they saw the Hira mountain (5:132–33; 58.35.208).

There are Muslims who have declared this incident to be an apparition rather than actual or factual. It is not actual or factual. However, the detail presented in this passage is specific. The Hira mountain is seen protruding between the two halves of the moon, which was probably reported to be low on the skyline. The relevant Quranic passage also warns against those who would declare the event to be but an illusion: such people deny the truth and follow their own lusts.

Another Tradition places the event historically. The note following this Hadith is explicit.

> Narrated Abdullah: Five (great events) have passed: the Smoke, the Moon. . . .
>
> [Translator's Note: The events referred to here are all mentioned in the Holy Quran. (a) the Smoke here means what the pagans of Mecca imagined to see in the sky because of their severe hunger when Allah afflicted them with famine. See 44:10; (b) The event of the splitting of the Moon which took place in the lifetime of the Prophet and was witnessed by the pagans, his companions and some believers. See (54:1)] (6:273–74; 60.225.290).

To my knowledge not one non-Islamic historical account attests to the splitting of the moon. This is significant. Such an occurrence would have amazed millions in various parts of the earth. Many historians of the seventh century would have written extensively of this event. Yet there is silence. The Muslim simply responds, "The Quran and Hadith affirm it, I believe it, that settles it."

A similar event affected Jews and Muslims:

> The sun stopped in the middle of the sky and delayed going down about a full day. There has never been a day like it before or since, a day when the Lord listened to a man. Surely the Lord was fighting for Israel. (Josh. 10:13–14)

Compare:

> Narrated Abu Huraira: So, the prophet carried out the expedition and when he reached that town at the time or nearly at the time of the Asr prayer, he said to the sun, "O sun! You are under Allah's Order and I am under Allah's Order. O Allah! Stop it (i.e. the sun) from setting." It was stopped till Allah made him victorious (4:226–27; 53.8.353).

Are we talking of illusions? Was there a miscalculation of time in the heat of battle? Was this an attempt by the authors to give God credit for a victory in battle against nonbelievers? Or . . . did it actually happen as recorded? And, if so, did it happen for the Jews or for the Muslims or for both?

How does the earth cease its rotation for a period of time? If the sun continued to shine, then people on the other side of the planet must have experienced prolonged darkness. Why is there no independent secular confirmation of these two events that would have so affected every inhabitant on the earth? These questions lead us to no confirmed and widely accepted conclusion. The faith response simply states that our all-powerful God can do as he pleases. With that the believer rests his case.

In the tradition of Elijah, Muhammad rebuked the drought and called down an abundance of rain.

> Narrated Anas Malik: Once in the lifetime of the Prophet the people were afflicted with drought (famine). While the Prophet was delivering the sermon on a Friday, a Bedouin stood up and said,

"O, Allah's Apostle! Our possessions are being destroyed and the children are hungry; Please invoke Allah (for rain)." So the Prophet raised his hands. At that time there was not a trace of a cloud in the sky. By Him in Whose Hands my soul is, as soon as he lowered his hands, clouds gathered like mountains, and before he got down from the pulpit, I saw the rain falling on the beard of the Prophet. It rained that day, the next day, the third day, the fourth day and until the next Friday. The same Bedouin or another man stood up and said, "O, Allah's Apostle! The houses have collapsed, our possessions and livestock have been drowned; Please invoke Allah (to protect us)." So the Prophet raised both his hands and said, "O Allah! Round about us and not on us." So, in whatever direction he pointed with his hands, the clouds dispersed and cleared away, and Medina's (sky) became clear as a hole in between the clouds. The valley of Qanat remained flooded for one month. None came from outside but that they talked about the abundant rain (2:26–27; 13.33.55).

Throughout history religious persons have been reputed to have performed miracles in regard to causing rain to fall. I recall a Baptist minister in Florida who told me of a Sunday morning when the rain plummeting against the church's tin roof was so loud that the noise blocked out the sound of his words. In his frustration he paused . . . and then in a loud and authoritative voice bellowed out a command to God to rebuke the rain and cause it to cease. Within a minute or two all was quiet and the sun began to shine. I was impressed with the story until the pastor, with a twinkle in his eye, went on to say he was emboldened by his knowledge that Florida rain showers are almost always severe as well as brief! It seems the pastor had more faith in his knowledge of meteorology than confidence in a prayer-answering God.

So-called miracle workers are prolific throughout the world. It is no small task to separate the genuine from the fraudulent. But, for the Muslim, there is no question but that the Prophet was a specially empowered man of God, a prophet not only of power but also of sensitivity. Muhammad's encounter with the weeping date-palm stem graphically illustrates the tender side of the Prophet's personality.

Narrated Jabir Abdullah: An Ansari woman said to Allah's Apostle, "O Allah's Apostle! Shall I make something for you to sit on, as I have a slave who is a carpenter?" He replied, "If you wish." So, she got a pulpit made for him. When it was Friday the Prophet sat on that pulpit. The date-palm stem near which the Prophet used to deliver his sermons cried so much so that it was about to burst. The Prophet came down from the pulpit to the stem and embraced it and it started groaning like a child being persuaded to stop crying and then it stopped crying. The Prophet said, "It has cried because of (missing) what it used to hear of religious knowledge" (3:174–75; 34.33.308).

One might be tempted to relegate this short story to the realm of bedtime stories specially written for Muslim children. Islam, however, strongly attests to the historicity of such events.

Anyone who has lived in the East knows of the vulnerability of slaves (servants) within the household where they labor. If any item is missing, suspicion immediately falls upon the househelp. In this Hadith, a helpless black slave attributes her deliverance to the intervention of Allah.

Narrated Aisha: A black lady slave of some of the Arabs embraced Islam and she had a hut in the mosque. She used to visit us and talk to us, and when she finished her talk, she used to say: "The day of the scarf was one of our Lord's wonders; Verily! He has delivered me from the land of Kufr." When she said the above verse many times, I (i.e. Aisha) asked her, "What was the day of the scarf?" She replied, "Once the daughter of some of my masters went out and she was wearing a leather scarf (round her neck) and the leather scarf fell from her and a hawk descended and picked it up, mistaking it for a piece of meat. They (i.e. my masters) accused me of stealing it and they tortured me to such an extent that they even looked for it in my private parts. So, while they all were around me, and I was in great distress, suddenly the hawk came over our heads and threw the scarf, and they took it. I said to them, 'This is what you accused me of stealing, though I was innocent'" (5:111–12; 58.25.176).

Within this chapter a number of miracles have been noted that have some measure of similarity with biblical events. Another of these parallels relates to an animal's speaking in a human voice. Numbers 22 has Balaam's donkey speaking a word of protest. The following Tradition highlights an incident in which a wolf carries on an intelligent conversation with an ungodly person.

This interaction directly led to the conversion of the heathen to Islam.

> Narrated Unais bin Amr: Ahban bin Aus said, "I was amongst my sheep. Suddenly a wolf caught a sheep and I shouted at it. The wolf sat on its tail and addressed me, saying, 'Who will look after it (i.e. the sheep) when you will be busy and not able to look after it? Do you forbid me the provision which Allah has provided me?'" Ahban added, "I clapped my hands and said, 'By Allah, I have never seen anything more curious and wonderful than this!' On that the wolf said, 'There is something (more curious) and wonderful than this: that is Allah's Apostle in those palm trees inviting people to Allah (i.e. Islam).'" Unais bin Amr further said, "Then Ahban went to Allah's Apostle and informed him what happened and embraced Islam" (3:298; 39.4.517).

Scoffers have ridiculed the Muslim belief that in a future day Allah will cause the sun to rise in the West. In a poetic style, the Prophet sets forth just such an eschatological event.

> Narrated Abu Dhar: The Prophet asked me at sunset, "Do you know where the sun goes (at the time of sunset)?" I replied, "Allah and His Apostle know better." He said, "It goes (i.e. travels) till it prostrates itself underneath the Throne, and takes the permission to rise again, and it is permitted and then (a time will come when) it will be about to prostrate itself but its prostration will not be accepted, and it will ask permission to go on its course, but it will not be permitted, but it will be ordered to return whence it has come and so it will rise in the west" (4:283; 54.4.421).

Thus concludes an overview of the significant recorded miracles that Muslim scholars have cited. In balance, one has to conclude that these events are hardly more incredible than those set forth in the Bible, though Christians are quick to point out that biblical miracles seem to have more purpose than those recorded in the Quran and Hadith.

It is right to discuss these Hadith citations with Muslims. Several will be completely unknown to the average follower of the Prophet. But be aware that the Bible actually records more specific and varied miracles than do the Quran and Hadith. Muslims may demand explanations of that which is inexplicable. Our best approach is to acknowledge that miracles do indeed occur and that God is capable of performing whatever is within his will. Then proceed to emphasize the greatest of all miracles of history, the incarnation, death, and resurrection of Christ.

rayer

erhaps 95 percent of Muslim adults worldwide do not follow the legalistic demands of orthodoxy in regard to the Islamic prayer ritual. I have met very few who are absolutely committed daily to arising before dawn and engaging in the first salat (prescribed prayer form). Most of the devout will pray upon waking from their night of rest, which will usually be some time after sunrise. Quite apart from timing, most Muslims simply are not inclined to commit themselves to the rigor of the five daily prayers. It is a massive struggle to do ablutions and perform the prostrations in a regulated manner in whatever circumstance one may find oneself. At school, at business, shopping, on holiday, during travel . . . whenever, wherever, the salat must be regularly and religiously performed. Most Muslims I know say they are unable to follow this Quranic command. They add that they are trusting Allah will be merciful and forgive them for their inadequacy.

There are exceptions, among them my close Muslim friend, Dr. Ali. Enduring the jests of some fellow academicians, he remains absolutely committed to the Islamic cycle of salat. Once, we were in a van returning from an outing. Suddenly, he became agitated. He kept looking for a place along the road where he could perform his prayers. Repeatedly, he requested the driver to stop and allow him to pray. The less religiously inclined Muslim at the wheel drove faster, seeking to more quickly deliver us to our destination. Upon arrival, Dr. Ali bolted out of the van and immediately commenced his salat. None of us can judge another's motivation, but after a decade of friendship with Dr. Ali, I cannot but conclude he is driven by a deep love for the Allah of his understanding. He would strongly affirm he finds prayer to be a privilege and a joy rather than a legalism to be endured.

Islam regards prayer as a sacrament of union between Allah and his creation. The salat embodies reverence and humility as well as perceived communication between God and man. Let us probe deeper into the theological dimensions of prayer as presented in the Hadith.

Theological Considerations

Muslim prayers are a duality expressed in form and content. The two are so interwoven that one could affirm that the medium is the message, or at least inseparable from it. Bowing, kneeling, and prostration are as integral to the efficacy of prayer as are the Quranic recitations that are repeated from memory during salat. Such a style of worship is observed in these words of Muhammad.

> Narrated Abdullah bin Umar: Whenever the Prophet came upon a mountain path or wasteland, he would say, "None has the right to be worshipped but Allah, alone who has no partner. All the kingdom belongs to Him and all the praises are for Him and He is omnipotent. We are returning with repentance, worshipping, prostrating ourselves and praising our Lord" (4:149; 52.133.238).

The unity of Allah is the foremost theological formulation of Islam. This unity is constantly emphasized in the Quran, the Hadith, and salat. Often it is framed in a negative context. "Who has no partner" is a direct refutation of the Trinity. According to their rational orientation Muslims cannot comprehend Jesus as fully God without ascribing partnership or duality to Allah. Thus they consistently make forceful objection to allowing Christ to assume any status other than that of a prophet. This belief is drilled into the Muslim mind by repetition each time salat is performed.

Allah, as the all-omnipotent One, is another basic theological emphasis in prayer. Man's response to God's power and authority is to simply bow low before him in submission and humility. The integration of form and content is seen in this interplay between posture and theology.

Personal salvation is important to Muslims. Their belief in the eternal existence of the soul is similar to that of Christians. So the salvific process is a key theme in all Islamic Scripture as well as in religious instruction.

The accumulation of merit is also an integral part of motivation for the regularized performance of salat.

> Narrated Abu Huraira: Allah's Apostle said, "The reward of the prayer offered by a person in congregation is twenty-five times greater than that of the prayer offered in one's house or in the market (alone). And this is because if he performs ablution and does it perfectly and then proceeds to the mosque with the sole intention of praying, then for every step he takes towards the mosque, he is upgraded one degree in reward and one sin is taken off (crossed out) from his accounts (of deeds)" (1:352; 10.30.620).

Huraira's Hadith highlights the role of prayer in obtaining forgiveness of sins; legalistic minutiae are indicated by the reference to steps taken toward the mosque. This tradition also emphasizes the community aspect of Islam. Merit is bestowed by the performance of salat within groups.

Muslims understand the interlinkage of the mosque and prayer. There is, however, an incongruity between doctrine and practice. Millions of Muslim women never step into a mosque for salat. For instance, among the sixty million Muslim women of Bangladesh, perhaps a few thousand have entered a mosque. But the teaching of Islam does not forbid women to pray in the mosque. In certain Islamic countries women are seen praying either in the rear or in the balcony of the mosque. If the commands of the Quran and Hadith apply equally to male and female, then why has a practice evolved wherein Muslim women often are limited to solitary prayer in the confines of their own homes? What about their appropriation of eternal merit such as that promised to those who pray in the mosque? These inconsistencies are usually missed by the average Muslim. Conversely, Muslims frequently allude to Islam's absolute commitment to sexual equality. Throughout my missionary career I have found it frustrating to meet dogmatic denials of these obvious, ongoing, and widespread realities.

Further emphasis to the mosque is given in this Hadith:

> Narrated Abu Huraira: The Prophet said, "When it is a Friday, the angels stand at the gate of the mosque and keep on writing the names of the persons coming to the mosque in succession according to their arrivals. The example of the one who enters the mosque in the earliest hour is that of one offering a camel (in sacrifice). The one coming next is like one offering a cow and then a ram and then a chicken and then an egg respectively. When the Imam comes out (for Jumu'a prayer) they (i.e. angels) fold their papers and listen to the Khutba (sermon)" (2:25; 13.29.51).

Here is an intense personalization of the function of angels. They are omnipresent beings particularly stationed at the entrance to mosques.

Cleansing, prayer, and forgiveness come together in this picturesque Tradition:

> Narrated Abu Huraira: I heard Allah's Apostle saying, "If there was a river at the door of anyone of you and he took a bath in it five times a day would you notice any dirt on him?" They said, "Not a trace of dirt would be left." The Prophet added, "That is the example of the five prayers with which Allah annuls evil deeds" (1:301; 10.6.506).

So the sacrament of prayer is efficacious for cancelling one's sins in the accounts that Allah maintains. In another Hadith this fact is reiterated with an additional requirement attached.

> Narrated Abu Huraira: Allah's Apostle said, "The angels keep on asking Allah's forgiveness for anyone of you, as long as he is at his Musalla (praying place) and he does not pass wind" (1:260; 8.61.436).

"Passing wind" being a disqualifying act illustrates the integration of the physical and the spiritual in Islam. The body is to be maximally clean during rites that link man to God. A Muslim friend was severely rebuked by his religious mother for touching the Quran without performing required ablutions. To the average Westerner, such meticulous obligations seem wearisome and even ludicrous. To the devout Muslim, they are acts of obedience that are not to be questioned.

Another down-to-earth Hadith leaves the reader wondering if Muslims accept these words in a figurative or a literal sense.

> Narrated Abdullah: A person was mentioned before the Prophet and he was told that he had kept on sleeping till morning and had not got up for prayer. The Prophet said, "Satan urinated in his ears" (2:135; 21.12.245).

The point is that the believer had his hearing silenced by an act of Satan that prevented him from hearing the morning call to prayer. Spiritually, the teaching is that Satan is continually active, seeking to negate the counsels of God. Many Muslims, however, would accept these words as they stand.

On a higher theological level, we find the Messenger giving this exhortation:

> Narrated Anas: Allah's Apostle said, "Whenever anyone of you invoke Allah for something, he should be firm in his asking, and he should not say: 'If you wish, give me . . .' for none can compel Allah to do something against His will" (9:418; 93.31.556).

So it is not necessary to petition conditionally. Allah will always operate within the perimeters of his will. Herein we see another teaching that leans toward fatalism. Prayer is simply getting ourselves and our desires in concert with the will of Allah. We accept that which God has preordained for us.

Prayer Forms

Muslim prayer, to be effective, must be preceded by ablutions; be at five specific times a day; include mandated Quranic verses; be said in certain postures; and be stated while the worshiper faces Mecca. The average Christian relishes the complete absence of such stipulations in his or her communion with God. The overwhelming majority of Muslims do not feel they have the prerogative to question these commands, as they are confident all prayer rituals are Allah-ordained. They may neglect salat but they never question the style that is mandated. Form *is* meaning to the Muslim.

Ablutions

Narrated Abu Abdullah: What has been revealed (regarding ablution)? The Statement of Allah: "O you who believe! When you intend to offer prayer, wash your faces and your forearms up to the elbows, rub (by passing wet hands over) your heads, and (wash) your feet up to the ankles." The Prophet had made clear that it is obligatory (while performing) ablutions to wash the (above mentioned) body parts once (1:101; 4.1.136).

This formula for washing is precisely followed by all Muslims worldwide. I have never encountered an aberration of any kind in my travels and interaction with Muslims. If water is not available, as was the case at certain times in the desert of Arabia, then sand is an acceptable substitute. What the Prophet has declared as obligatory must stand forever.

The attention paid to meticulous detail is alluded to in this Tradition:

Narrated Abu Huraira: Allah's Apostle said, "Whoever cleans his private parts with stones should do so with odd numbers. And whoever wakes up from his sleep should wash his hands before putting them in the water for ablution, because nobody knows where his hands were during sleep" (1:114; 4.26.163).

Cleansing with stones following defecation was a practice made necessary because of a scarcity of water. The command to use odd numbers seems to be pure superstition. If the Muslim touched his genitals during sleep, this would cause spiritual impurity and would need to be negated by washing. So many of these legalisms seem to be directed toward male rather than female believers. The male bias throughout the Quran and Hadith must be understood in a cultural context wherein men were the dominant influence in all areas of society. This sociological phenomenon has been preserved in Islam throughout the centuries.

Further legalisms define the occasions on which ablutions must be repeated.

> Narrated Ata: "If a worm comes out of one's anus or if a drop of discharge equal to the size of a louse comes out of one's penis (then it is essential to repeat the ablution.)" Abdullah said, "If one laughs in prayer, he must repeat his prayer and not the ablution." Al-Hasan said, "If someone takes out (cuts) some of his hair, cuts his nails or removes his leather socks, he is not to repeat his ablution" (1:121; 4.35.175).

By what criteria, it could be asked, are regulations set forth for physical purity before Allah? What does a worm exiting the anus or measuring one's seminal discharge have to do with spirituality? Why relate being freed from repeating ablutions to cutting one's nails or removing one's socks? These minutiae seem to exceed the legalisms of the Pharisees.

Yet, we find Muslims thanking Allah for revealing these directives that clearly define the will of God for even the smallest details of life. These Hadith contribute to the reality of Islam as a total code of life for believers. Christians tend to ridicule such a straightjacket of regulation and deem it an interference in areas of personal choice and freedom. In these two approaches one clearly sees the dichotomy between law and grace.

The Call to Prayer

For millions of Muslims, the call to five times of daily prayer is a melodious summons from Allah requesting (and commanding) his people to pause for a ten-minute interaction between the Creator and the created. This ritual was inaugurated in the time of the Prophet.

> Narrated Ibn Umar: When the Muslims arrived at Medina, they used to assemble for prayer, and used to guess the time for it. During those days, the practice of Adhan [call to prayer] for the prayers had not yet been introduced. One time they discussed this problem regarding the call for prayer. Some people suggested the use of a bell like the Christians, others proposed a trumpet like the horn used by the Jews, but Umar was the first to suggest that a man should call (the people) for prayer; so Allah's Apostle ordered Bilal

to get up and pronounce the Adhan for prayers (1:334–35;
11.1.578).

Narrated Anas Malik: The Prophet said, "Straighten your rows as
the straightening of rows is essential for perfect and correct prayer"
(1:388; 11.73.690).

Perhaps one of the most disciplined moments among Muslims
occurs at the time of forming lines just preceding salat. I have
stood on the top of a building and watched thousands of believers within seconds fold into perfectly straight rows. They seem to
automatically measure distances on both sides as well as in front
and back. The resulting symmetry is at times awesome. All of this
is done in the interest of legalistically fulfilling the requirements
of Islam.

Prostration

Another absolute in form ritual is prostration, the precedent
for which is established by Muhammad and David:

Narrated Al-Awwam: I asked Mujahid regarding the prostration
in Surat Sad. He said, "I asked Ibn Abbas, 'What evidence makes
you prostrate?' He said, 'Don't you recite: *And among his prog-
eny, David and Solomon . . .* (Quran 6:85) *Those are they whom
Allah guided. So follow their guidance.* (Quran 6:91)

So David was the one of those (prophets) whom Prophet (Muhammad) was ordered to follow. David prostrated, so Allah's Apostle
(Muhammad) performed this prostration too'" (4:312; 60.248.331).

I have always been impressed with the reverential beauty and
sublimity illustrated by a great mass of people bowing with faces
to the ground in prayerful adoration of their Creator. The form
is specifically biblical and so much richer than the typical Christian's casual posture of sitting in a cushioned pew with legs
crossed while listening to the prayers of a minister. We as biblical Christians would do well to regain that which we have lost
down through the centuries. A humble posture of kneeling or
prostration may assist in rediscovering an attitude of awe and

reverence in the presence of the exalted Lord and sovereign of the universe.

The exception to the requirement to prostrate oneself relates to old age:

> Narrated Aisha: The Prophet used to offer prayer at night (for such a long time) that his feet used to crack. I said, "O Allah's Apostle Why do you do it since Allah has forgiven you your faults of the past and those to follow?" He said, "Shouldn't I love to be a thankful slave (of Allah)?" When he became old, he prayed while sitting, but if he wanted to perform a bowing, he would get up, recite (some other verses) and then perform the bowing (6:344–45; 60.272.361).

It would seem that few elderly Muslims follow this precedent of Muhammad. I have never seen a Muslim pray salat while seated. But this form may be utilized by the infirm in the privacy of their homes.

This Tradition highlights what is affirmed repeatedly throughout Al-Bukhari's compilation of the acts of the Prophet. Muhammad was reputed to be a man engaged in an intense quest to be a humble worshiper of Allah. His attitude of mind before his Sovereign was said to be that of a thankful slave. There have been innumerable attempts to reconcile this apparent spiritual desire with the fact that Muhammad never became a believer in Christ as God, but instead was the instrument used to develop a distinctively anti-Christian theology. Without doubt, this seeming contradiction has bothered me more than any other facet of the Prophet's life. I await a day of fuller understanding when these types of obscurities will be enfolded into complete revelation.

Concentration and Dealing with Interruptions to Prayer

Muhammad's concentration in prayer is emphasized by this narrator:

> Abdullah stated: While the Prophet was in the state of prostration, surrounded by a group of people from Quraish pagans, 'Uqba bin Abi Muait came and brought the intestines of a camel and threw them on the back of the Prophet. The Prophet did not raise his head from prostration till Fatima (i.e. his daughter) came and

removed those intestines from his back, and invoked evil on whoever had done (the evil deed). The Prophet said, "O Allah! Destroy
the chiefs of Quraish" (4:274; 53.40.409).

This was a case of extreme provocation. Raw, red intestines of
a common camel had been thrust upon Muhammad's back as he
reverently prostrated himself in prayer. His refusal to interrupt
his communion with Allah has been cited as an example for the
faithful to follow. Hence, Muslims will almost never deviate from
their salat ritual once it has commenced. The evolution of this
regulation is seen in this Tradition.

> Narrated Abdullah: We used to greet the Prophet while he was
> praying, and he used to reply to our greetings. But when we came
> back from Najashi (the king of Ethiopia) we greeted him (while
> he was praying) and he did not reply to us. We said, "O Allah's
> Apostle! We used to greet you in the past and you used to reply to
> us." He said, "Verily! The mind is occupied and busy with more
> important matters during prayer" (So one cannot return greetings)
> (5:137; 58.36.215).

There is, however, a Hadith that allows for an interruption during
prayer.

> Narrated Abu Al-Khudri: The Prophet said, "If, while you are pray-
> ing, somebody intends to pass in front of you, prevent him; and
> should he insist, prevent him again; and if he insists again, fight
> with him (i.e. prevent him violently e.g. by pushing him violently),
> because such a person is (like) a devil" (4:319; 54.10.495).

One must remember that Muslims pray with their eyes open.
Therefore mirrors and pictures must not be placed so the worshiper
is distracted by these or other items. (For example, Dr. Ali covers
his wife's dresser mirror at prayer time.) Still, it is hard to imagine
a violent shoving match breaking out because a person has passed
in front of a worshiping Muslim. Such legalisms appear to be
excessive.

Two further Hadith continue along these lines.

> Narrated Anas: The Prophet said, "Whenever anyone of you is in
> prayer, he is speaking in private to his Lord and so he should

neither spit in front of him nor on his right side but to his left side under his left foot" (2:171; 22.12.305).

Narrated Anas: The Prophet said, "If anyone of you feels drowsy while praying, he should sleep till he understands what he is saying (reciting)" (1:139; 4.55.212).

Allah is given the place of honor by being deemed to be in front of or to the right of the worshiper. The left side carries much the same connotation as one finds in our Scripture. The right side is the place of honor while the left implies either less recognition or even a place of judgment. It is interesting to note that drowsiness is a legitimate reason to postpone salat. This indicates that the substance of prayer is more important than the form.

Muhammad concluded that any obstruction to prayer has its origin in Satanic activity. He is persistent and effective. We see a similarity to the reference to Satan moving to and fro throughout the world seeking whom he may devour (1 Pet. 5:8). In this colorful Tradition we see more of spiritual warfare according to Islamic belief.

Narrated Abu Huraira: Allah's Apostle said, "When the Adhan is pronounced Satan takes to his heels and passes wind with noise during his flight in order not to hear the Adhan. When the Adhan is completed he comes back and again takes to his heels when the Iqama [recitation] is pronounced and after its completion he returns again till he whispers into the heart of the person (to divert his attention from his prayer) and makes him remember things which he does not recall to his mind before the prayer and that causes him to forget how much he has prayed" (1:336; 11.4.582).

Anthropomorphic references to heavenly beings create somewhat of a problem for many Muslims. Islamic theology declares God, angels, *jinn,* and Satan to be spirit. Yet, in the Quran, Allah is declared to see, hear, speak, and walk. Angels have sight and can write. Jinn assume many different forms and perform various acts, both constructive and destructive. In this passage we see Satan fleeing, passing wind, and whispering. I have had an Egyptian fundamentalist Muslim become angrily frustrated when he tried to reconcile to me the spirit-cum-physical aspects of Allah. This conflict has opened opportunities for me to give witness to the ultimate anthropomorphism, as declared by our Scripture, to be God assuming the form of man in the person of Jesus Christ.

Principles of Orderly Worship

The Hadith exhorts believers to engage in orderly worship and to avoid excessive emotionalism.

> Narrated Abu Musa Al-Ashari: We were in the company of Allah's Apostle (during Hajj). Whenever we went up to a high place we used to say: "None has the right to be worshipped but Allah, and Allah is Greater," and our voices used to rise, so the Prophet said, "O people! Be merciful to yourselves (i.e. don't raise your voice), for you are not calling a deaf or an absent one, but One who is with you, and no doubt He is Hearer, Nigh" (4:148; 52.131.235).

In a number of Sufi-oriented gatherings of Muslims, I have observed a great deal of emotional worship. Especially in *dhikr* (corporate recitation of religious terms) one finds outbursts of exuberance in worship. These expressions of emotion, however, are the exception rather than the norm within Islam.

I have never seen Muslim women clapping in a mosque. But this Tradition gives the imprimatur of Muhammad for the practice.

> Narrated Abu Huraira: The Prophet said, "The saying 'Subhan Allah' [Holiness be to God] is for men and clapping is for women. (If something happens in the prayer, the men can invite the attention of the Imam by saying 'Subhan Allah' and the women, by clapping their hands)" (2:165; 22.5.295).

The Prophet was praised for his consideration of some believers who could not endure lengthy prayers.

> Narrated Abu Masud: A man came to the Prophet and said: "I keep away from the morning prayer only because such and such person prolongs the prayer when he leads us in it." The narrator added: I had never seen Allah's Apostle more furious in giving advice than he was on that day. He said, "O people! There are some among you who make others dislike good deeds and cause the others to have aversion to congregational prayers. Beware! Whoever among you leads the people in prayer should not pro-

long it, because among them there are the sick, the old, and the needy" (8:84; 72.75.131).

For the Muslim, prayer is a vital focus of life. One can only imagine how communion with our Lord would be enhanced by pausing ten minutes five times a day to bow in meaningful worship and prayer to our Creator-Sustainer. Stripped of its legalisms and theological aberrations, perhaps the ideal of Muslim prayer has a challenge for the devout Christian. Certainly Muslims deeply appreciate being prayed for. Prayer can be an effective catalyst between the religious distinctives of Islam and Christianity.

6

Fasting

As I write this chapter I am living surrounded by fasting
Muslims. Each morning at 2:30 the "callers" move
through the deserted streets crying out loudly for all
the faithful to arise, cook, eat, and pray before enough light pierces
the predawn darkness to allow one to distinguish a black thread
from a white one.

> Narrated Sahl bin Sad: "Some people who intended to fast tied
> black and white threads to their legs and went on eating till they
> differentiated between the two" (3:78; 31.16.141).

Having kept the complete Muslim fast on two occasions, I can
testify to the rigors of the practice. Such an exercise of abstinence
requires great discipline. The believer is not allowed to eat, drink,
smoke, or have sexual relations from approximately one hour
before sunrise until the precise moment of sunset for the entire
lunar month of Ramadan. Very early in the day the body begins
to crave liquids. Especially in tropical climates one experiences
rather severe discomfort throughout the month. The final ten days
are the most difficult.

It is extremely difficult to be a totally faithful Muslim. Praying
five times each day and keeping the fast are physical and spiritual disciplines that test one's endurance to the limit. One won-

ders how many adherents would there be if evangelical Christianity had such obligations for the faithful.

To the Muslim, fasting is equated with obedience to one of the pillars of Islam. The Quran and Hadith command and commend physical abstinence to believers. All in the household of Islam believe in the practice and perhaps half of all Muslim adults fulfill the requirements of the total month of fasting. Admittedly, such an estimate is at best a guess based on limited empirical and written data. Many start the fast and do not complete it. Others covertly snack throughout the day. Still others have legitimate and sanctioned reasons for breaking the fast. There is also a great deal of variance from country to country. In certain Islamic nations, publicly breaking the fast is a criminal offense punishable by a prison term. In countries where Muslims are a small minority few strictly adhere to the prohibitions.

Many colorful and descriptive comments about the fast are contained in the Hadith.

> Narrated Abu Huraira: Allah's Apostle said, "When the month of Ramadan comes, the gates of Paradise are opened and the gates of (Hell) Fire are closed, and the devils are chained" (4:320; 54.10.497).

It would be interesting to know what Muhammad meant by this statement. I have never observed anything in the Muslim world that would lead me to conclude that devils are chained during the month of fasting. Conversely, I have actually seen more anger and quarreling among the believers during this time than in any other month of the year. During Ramadan Muslims never paused from the grotesque practice of killing fellow Muslims in the protracted Iran-Iraq war. It would also seem the fanatical fringe element of religious Islam is more active in Ramadan than at any other time of the year. As I write these words three women missionaries and two small children have just been kidnaped by Muslims on a small island in the country where I am resident. The abductors are demanding an eighty-thousand-dollar ransom. We are presently at the midpoint of the fast.

Reasons for Fasting

One dialogue has as its foundation the accumulation of merit inherent in the act of fasting:

> Narrated Abdullah bin Amr: Allah's Apostle was informed that I used to say: "By Allah, I will fast all the days and pray all the nights as long as I live." On that, Allah's Apostle asked me, "Are you the one who says: 'I will fast all the days and pray all the nights as long as I live?'" I said, "Yes, I have said it." He said, "You cannot do that. So fast (sometimes) and do not fast (sometimes). Pray and sleep. Fast for three days a month, for the reward of a good deed is multiplied by ten times, and so the fasting of three days a month equals the fasting of a year." I said, "O Allah's Apostle! I can fast more than this." He said, "Fast on alternate days as this was the fasting of David which is the most moderate sort of fasting." I said, "O Allah's Apostle! I can fast more than that." He said, "There is nothing better than that" (4:416; 55.33.629).

There are many references in the Hadith to rewards accrued by participation in the Ramadan fast:

> Narrated Abu Said: I heard the Prophet saying, "Indeed, anyone who fasts for one day for Allah's pleasure, Allah will keep his face away from (Hell) fire for (a distance covered by a journey of) seventy years" (4:66; 52.36.93).

Numbers of days and years often are referred to in passages that discuss merit. There will be an equation between a day of good works and the resulting years of deliverance from hell.

The performance of meritorious acts also leads to the forgiveness of one's sins.

> Narrated Abu Huraira: Allah's Apostle said, "Whoever observes fasts during the month of Ramadan out of sincere faith, and hoping to attain Allah's rewards, then all his past sins will be forgiven" (1:34; 2.29.37).

Islamic theology does not exactly authenticate this Hadith. More than fasting is involved in receiving the forgiveness of all past sin. Islam presents a wide range of legalistic works that must be accomplished in order to have one's sins forgiven. Fasting is only one of these.

Missing a day of fasting is common among Muslims. But this Hadith shows the seriousness of such an omission.

> Narrated Abu Huraira from the Prophet: "Whoever did not fast for one day of Ramadan without a genuine excuse or a disease, then even if he fasted for a complete year, it would not compensate for that day" (3:88; 31.29.155).

The gravity of this problem is simply not accepted by most Muslims. In one Islamic country, roadside shanty restaurants are made obscure by discreetly positioning a sheet across the doorway. Inside, Muslims engage in animated conversation while eating, drinking, and smoking. In this particular nation, seldom do the religious leaders protest this nonreligious behavior.

Muhammad quotes Allah as his authority for the following exhortation.

> Narrated Abu Huraira, The Prophet said, "Allah said: 'The Fast is for Me and I will give a reward for it, as he (the one who observes the fast) leaves his sexual desire, food and drink for My sake. Fasting is a screen (from Hell) and there are two joys for a fasting person, one at the time of breaking his fast, and the second at the time when he will meet his Lord'" (9:434; 93.35.584).

Here fasting is linked with deprivation, rewards, and joy. I can concur with the statement concerning the elation that occurs each evening when the fast in completed. It is a special privilege to end the fourteen-hour day of abstinence with my fasting Muslim friends. How we all relish that first prolonged drink of lemonade.

Regulations for Fasting

Generally speaking, there is a law or an opinion in Islam to cover every human activity. Myths, legends, and scholarly opinions all contribute to the regulations on Muslim fasting. In this section, I will highlight a few of the Traditions the Islamic community regards as important.

Narrated Abu Huraira: The Prophet said, "If somebody eats or
drinks forgetfully then he should complete his fast, for what he has
eaten or drunk has been given to him by Allah" (3:85; 31.26.154).

There is allowance in Islam for the unintentional fault committed
by the sincere believer. More often than not the permission is
followed by a statement of rationalization.

Ibn Abbas used to say, "Allah's Apostle fasted and sometimes did
not fast while travelling, so one may fast or not (on journeys)"
(5:401; 59.46.576).

Once again it is clearly seen that the apostle's behavior is to
be the regulatory precedent that governs Muslims in all places
and in all ages. When one thinks of travel in seventh-century Arabia, one must understand there was a lack of air-conditioned Mer-
cedes-Benzes. Riding a camel through the desert in a howling
sandstorm and searing heat does not lend itself to an all-day deprivation of food and water. Thus, the optional nature of this Hadith.

Advice on sex is liberally scattered through the Traditions. It
would seem to have been one of the favorite subjects of the com-
pilers of the Hadith. There are strict Islamic regulations against
having sexual intercourse while fasting.

*"It is made lawful for you to go unto your wives on the night of
the fast. They are raiment for you and ye are raiment for them.
Allah is aware that ye were deceiving yourselves in this respect
and He hath turned in mercy toward you and relieved you. So hold
intercourse with them and seek that which Allah hath ordained
for you, and eat and drink until the white thread becometh distinct to you from the black thread of the dawn. Then strictly observe
the fast till nightfall and touch them not, but be at your devotions
in the mosques. These are the limits imposed by Allah, so approach
them not."* [underlining added] (Quran 2:187)

In one of the most obvious contradictions between the Quran and
the reported activity of the Prophet, we have this account by
Muhammad's favorite wife, Aisha.

Narrated Aisha: "The Prophet used to kiss and embrace (his wives) while he was fasting, and he had more power to control his desires than any of you" (3:82; 31.23.149).

The Quran forbids touching one's wives during the fast, yet the Prophet kisses and touches his wives. It is inferred that he stopped short of intercourse during these fasting hours. I have never heard a scholar of Islam attempt to reconcile these two statements.

The relationship between fasting and the sex drive is also addressed in the Traditions.

Narrated Alqama: The Prophet said: "He who can afford to marry should marry, because it will help him refrain from looking at other women, and save his private parts from committing illegal sexual relation; and he who cannot afford to marry is advised to fast, as fasting will diminish his sexual power" (3:72; 31.10.129).

Bodily weakness is a definite part of the fasting process. Early into the month the energy level begins to dissipate. The brain functions at a slower pace. The sex drive also decreases. Thus, Muhammad recommends fasting as an alternative to be considered by those who cannot afford marriage yet need to control their sexual urges. The practical question arises as to how long a person could continue such a fast.

Forgetfully eating and drinking during the fast is not to be penalized. The same is true concerning having sex.

Al-Hasan and Mujahid said, "If one has sexual intercourse for-getfully, then no penalty will be imposed on him" (3:85; 31.26.153).

One cannot help but notice these directives are almost always male-oriented and directed. Females are not expected to be initiators in sexual relations, therefore they are peripheral to the regulations.

I have frequently pondered how Muslim women must feel when they read a statement by the Prophet that appears to demean them.

Narrated Abu Said: The Prophet said, "Isn't it true that a woman does not pray and does not fast while menstruating? And that is the defect (loss) in her religion" (3:98; 31.41.172).

During the fast there will normally be a time when a female will menstruate. Her body at that time is considered physically impure and therefore spiritually unfit to approach Allah in the intensely religious rituals of prayer and fasting. Muhammad declares this to be a religious defect in women. As my mind recoils at such a hurtful statement, I have to be fair and admit the Old Testament law also regarded menstruating women to be unclean. There is no allusion to such a time of female impurity under the dispensation of grace in the New Testament.

An often quoted Tradition relates to the smell of the breath of the person keeping the fast.

> Narrated Abu Huraira: The Prophet said, "By Him in Whose Hands my soul is, the smell coming out from the mouth of a fasting person is better in the sight of Allah than the smell of musk" (3:66; 31.2.118).

Perhaps Allah enjoys the smell but many people find such breath offensive. For the ascetically minded, there is always the option of brushing one's teeth four or five times a day. Most Muslims find the trouble and expense of that option to be quite unnecessary. My friends speak appreciatively of the smell of the breath of fasting Muslims.

Muhammad, however, gave an example to his followers concerning brushing one's teeth during Ramadan.

> Anas said, "It is mentioned that the Prophet cleaned his teeth with a siwak (twig of a tree) while fasting, and Ibn Umar used to clean his teeth with Siwak in the early and the late hours of the day without swallowing the resultant saliva (while fasting)." Said Ata, "The swallowing of saliva does not break the fast" (3:84; 31.25.151).

Throughout the Muslim world the fast is a time of voluminous spitting. Office walls are filled with slowly dripping saliva. Corridors are slimy. The air is filled with the unsavory noise of throats being cleared and spit being thrust out of open mouths. Prudence demands great care in walking about in a Muslim country during Ramadan lest one inadvertently fall into the trajectory of a moist projectile. Most Muslims realize they are allowed to swallow their saliva while fasting. But many seem to enjoy making a public display of their piety by going beyond the demands of their law.

Even flies do not escape the scrutiny of the Hadith.

> Al-Hasan said, "If a fly enters one's throat (while one is fasting), there is no harm in it" (3:85; 31.26.153).

One final citation from the Hadith pulls together the spiritual ideal for the Ramadan fast:

> Narrated Abu Huraira: Allah's Apostle said, "Fasting is a shield or protection from the fire and from committing sins. If one of you is fasting, he should avoid sexual relation with his wife and quarrelling, and if somebody should fight or quarrel with him, he should say, 'I am fasting'" (3:71; 31.9.128).

Is it profitable to fast for one month during daylight hours? Can the ideal of purity be attained? Does the fast assist in the development of a real hunger for God? Are Muslims demonstratively better people for enduring a month of deprivation? It is probably impossible to give a comprehensive answer to these questions. There are too many variables as different cultures and individuals are evaluated. The Muslim will fervently defend the fast. But that may stem more from the perspective of obedience to Allah's command than from an empirical analysis of benefits accrued to Islamic society in general and to the individual believer in particular. Actually, a pillar of Islam is simply not vulnerable to critique or evaluation. As long as Islam endures, there will be a Ramadan fast to observe.

Should Christians living among Muslims observe and follow the rituals of the fast? This is a most controversial subject. Having followed the Muslim style of fasting, I can state it was deeply appreciated by my friends that I, a Christian, would endure personal deprivation as they were doing. Other missionaries I know have testified of new friendships that were gained as a result of keeping the fast.

Observing the fast should not be legalistically demanded of any Christian. However, it is my opinion that it should not be prohibited. The arguments set forth by those adamantly opposed to any Christian's following the Muslim form of fasting seem to me to be rather inadequate.

The follower of Christ will need to explain that his motivation for keeping the Ramadan fast is in the area of identification and for the purpose of developing a deeper understanding of Islam. Differences between the legalisms of Islam and the optional varieties of biblical fasting should be enunciated. Above all, the Christian should make the month a concentrated time of seeking God in a new and fresh manner. It is quite possible that this combination will be a powerful testimony to onlooking Muslims.

7

Pilgrimage

indus to Benares, Christians and Jews to Jerusalem,
Bahais to Haifa, Shiites to Karbala, Sunnis to Mecca.
I took a course at Harvard University on "Pilgrimages."
The material included all of the preceding plus a slide-illustrated
presentation of John Bunyan's *Pilgrim's Progress*. There is a deep
desire within the heart of religiously inclined people to personally
visit sacred cities, shrines, and rivers that play a significant part in
their spiritual quest.

Julie and I went to Israel in 1972. What powerful emotional
reactions we experienced as we visited the Temple Mount, Geth-
semane, Tiberias, Galilee, and Haifa. Crossing the Galilee in a
small launch evoked vivid memories of our Savior's ministry in
and around one of the more beautiful lakes of the world. Eating
"Saint Peter's fish" in a quaint lakeside restaurant gave a sense
of the reality of biblical geography that could never be found in
pages of a book. The trip was a highlight of our lives. Now, many
years later, we long to return for another visit. We had become
satisfied participants in a religious pilgrimage.

Origins of the Hajj

The pilgrimage (Hajj) most assuredly is an emotional and spiritual highlight of Muslims' lives. But, in addition, it is an obliga-

tion to be fulfilled in response to commands found in the Quran and Hadith. In the time of Muhammad, new converts to Islam questioned the appropriateness of following a custom that was heathen in nature. It took a direct revelation from Allah to authenticate the practice.

> Narrated Asim bin Sulaiman: I asked Anas bin Malik about Safa and Marwa. Anas replied, "We used to consider (i.e. going around) them a custom of the pre-Islamic period of Ignorance, so when Islam came, we gave up going around them." Then Allah revealed:
>
> > Verily, Safa and Marwa (i.e. two mountains at Mecca) are among the Symbols of Allah. It is therefore no sin for the one who performs the Hajj of the House (of Allah) or performs the Umra to ambulate (Tawaf) between them (Quran 2:158) (6:21; 60.21.23).

The non-Muslim world has asked Islamic theologians hard questions concerning the Hajj. In a religion so adamantly opposed to any form of idolatry, how can it permit any earthly place to assume gigantic spiritual proportions? A cubical building (Kaaba) housing a holy Black Stone has become the focus of all worshiping Muslims worldwide. Circumambulation of the Kaaba and kissing the stone appear to the dispassionate observer to be idolatrous acts. To make a pilgrimage of thousands of miles to enter into such a prescribed ceremony can be understood only through the mind and heart of the nonquestioning believer. I find it impossible to comprehend millions of Muslims each year bowing before a stone and kissing it in a spirit of spiritual ecstasy. The rock was being worn down by human touch, so it now has been covered and the devout kiss the covering.

The stone's origin is lost in historical obscurity. Modern scholarship proclaims its probable genesis as a meteorite. Pilgrims care little for such academic questions. They are emotionally overwhelmed by an intense spiritual euphoria as they move into proximity to the Kaaba and the holy Black Stone.

There was a great contrast between the pagan and the Islamic Hajj.

> Abu Huraira said, "Abu Bakr sent me in that Hajj in which he was the chief of the pilgrims along with the announcers whom he sent on the Day of Nahr to announce at Mina. 'No pagan shall perform

Hajj after this year, and none shall perform the Tawaf [circum-ambulation] around the Kaaba in a naked state'" (6:144; 60.137.179).

It is difficult to imagine a day when this ritual was performed by naked people, although a number of Hadith refer to this pre-Islamic custom. Muslims engage in Hajj rites in conservative robes. There is no distinction between rich and poor.

In Saudi Arabia all non-Muslims are regarded as pagans and thus are prohibited from even visiting the holy city of Mecca, the centerpiece of pure Islam. Planes are prohibited from flying over Mecca for fear the presence of nonbelievers on the aircraft will pollute the purity of the city. Interestingly, the greatest and most embarrassing problem in Mecca occurred when rival Muslim groups went so far as to have a shootout within the sacred precinct of the Kaaba mosque. The Hadith speaks to this possibility.

> Narrated Al-Maqburi: I saw with my own eyes the Prophet when he, after glorifying and praising Allah, started saying, "Allah, not the people, made Mecca a sanctuary, so anybody who has belief in Allah and the Last Day should neither shed blood in it, nor should he cut down its trees. If anybody tells (argues) that fighting in it is permissible on the basis that Allah's Apostle did fight in Mecca, say to him, 'Allah allowed His Apostle and did not allow you'" (3:36; 29.8.58).

Muhammad was allowed to do battle in Mecca because the city needed to be liberated from the pagans. He was to turn Mecca into a place of holiness, peace, and refuge for the faithful. Sad to say, Muslim political antagonisms have often spilled over into one of the most intensely religious cities on earth.

> Narrated Ibn Abbas: The Prophet said, "Allah has made this place (Mecca) a sanctuary since the creation of the heavens and the earth and will remain a sanctuary until the Day of Resurrection as Allah has ordained its sanctity [sacredness]" (3:38; 29.10.60).

If Allah truly guaranteed the sanctity of Mecca up to the day of resurrection, the obvious question is, what happened along the way? To a Muslim, the commands of God are absolute and cannot be countermanded. Therefore, how is it possible for Iranian

Muslims to desecrate Mecca by initiating a gun battle within the holy Kaaba? The Arab Muslim would likely respond by saying such men are infidels. This is a defensive position taken by people of most religions when they are embarrassed by the actions of those from within their community. They simply deny the religious credentials of the wrongdoer. By this act, the purity of God and his revelation is preserved while the blame is allowed to fall on the hypocrite. But the pertinent question still remains as to whether a reprobate can negate what Allah has ordained. Seemingly so.

The activity of Abraham and Muhammad are seen in this Tradition.

> Narrated Abdullah bin Zaid: The Prophet said, "The Prophet Abraham made Mecca a sanctuary, and asked for Allah's blessing in it. I made Medina a sanctuary as Abraham made Mecca a sanctuary and I asked for Allah's blessing in its measures" (3:192–93; 34.54.339).

Mecca, Medina, and Jerusalem rate as the three most holy cities of Islam. A full-orbed pilgrimage would include a visit to each of these places. Medina has been made especially holy because the grave of Muhammad is within the city.

Muhammad cleansed the Kaaba of idols, but he did not destroy it. Seemingly he was sensitive to the religious feelings of converts to Islam who had held the Kaaba in such high esteem.

> Narrated Aisha: Allah's Apostle said to me, "Were your people not close to the pre-Islamic period of ignorance, I would have demolished the Kaaba and would have rebuilt it on its original foundations laid by Abraham (for Quraish had curtailed its building), and I would have built a back door (too)" (2:383; 26.41.655).

The belief in Abraham's role in this sacred place of worship assured its continuity within Islam throughout the ensuing centuries. Further detail is fleshed out in this Hadith:

> Narrated Ibn Abbas: When Allah's apostle arrived in Mecca, he refused to enter the Kaaba while there were idols in it. So he ordered that they be taken out. The pictures of the (Prophets) Abraham and Ishmael, holding arrows of divination in their hands, were carried out. The Prophet said, "May Allah ruin them (i.e. the infi-

dels) for they knew very well that they (i.e. Abraham and Ishmael)
never drew lots by these (divination arrows)" (5:406; 59.47.584).

The interesting point here is the role Abraham and Ishmael had
in the pre-Islamic Kaaba. Where did their pictures come from?
How did they become related to the concept of divination in the
minds of the infidels? Muhammad was quick to denounce the
supposed association of the prophets with magical phenomena.

A prophecy concerning the Kaaba has been of special interest
to Muslims.

> Aisha said that the Prophet said, "An (Ethiopian) army will attack
> the Kaaba and that army will sink down in the earth" (2:390;
> 26.48.664).

I am not aware of any such attack by the Ethiopians, much less a
historical reference to an army sinking into the earth. This
happening may best be explained by Islamic theologians affirming
it as eschatological in nature. It is true that this Hadith is framed
in the future tense.

Rituals of the Hajj

Al-Bukhari Hadith does not go into any significant detail
regarding the Hajj ritual. Other traditions and commentaries
speak more elaborately to the subject. There are, however, a few
specific instructions given for the benefit of believers.

Kissing the Black Stone is central to Hajj ritual. The theology
of the stone is briefly summarized in this Hadith.

> Narrated Abis bin Rabi'a: Umar came near the Black Stone and
> kissed it and said, "No doubt, I know that you are a stone and can
> neither benefit anyone nor harm anyone. Had I not seen Allah's
> Apostle kissing you I would not have kissed you" (2:390–91;
> 26.49.667).

The stone is not thought to be a purveyor of magical power. In
fact, its status is neutral. It can neither harm nor benefit the
worshiper. There seemed to be perplexity in the mind of Umar.
How can a monotheistic view of God so opposed to idols of

rock reconcile with the kissing of the stone? His response seemed to be explanation of last resort. Umar thoroughly trusted the judgment of the Prophet. Therefore, the act of kissing the rock is simply following the example of the founder of Islam. It is an act of faith, even when it seemingly contradicts other revelation.

I wonder what Muhammad, if he were alive today, would say about the overt and blatant worship of the rock by millions of Muslims. Without doubt many, like Umar, kiss the rock with no thought of worship. But, knowing folk Islam as I do, the Black Stone encourages animistic practice. I wonder what would happen if a strong and respected reformer advocated removal of the stone from the Kaaba. Probably this could never happen; the example of the Prophet gives precedent for leaving the stone in the Kaaba.

> Narrated Ibn Umar: A man asked the Prophet: "What (kinds of clothes) should a Muhrim (a Muslim intending to perform Hajj) wear?" He replied, "He should not wear a shirt, a turban, trousers, a headcloak or a garment scented with saffron or Wars (kinds of perfumes). And if he has no slippers, then he can use Khuffs (leather socks) but the socks should be cut short so as to make the ankles bare" (1:99–100; 3.54.136).

The point of prescribed dress for the pilgrims is egalitarianism. The rich and the poor become indistinguishable. All are humbled before Allah. For a moment in space and time the *Hajjis* no longer appear as slaves or potentates. They look, smell, and act as one. It is but a brief interlude from reality. Although according to the Quran Islam is casteless, the truth is far different. Would a street sweeper dare have a friendship with a rich merchant? If a daughter of a Muslim judge falls in love with an illiterate carpenter, one can rest assured they will never be allowed to marry. Even shades of skin color lead to divisiveness. A wealthy young Indian businessman who is seeking a wife will demand a very fair-skinned maiden. Girls of dark complexion face difficulty in finding a husband of choice. So the Hajj and its claim of universal Islamic oneness is undercut in the initial instance, on the individual level. Then, a case can be made that this disunity extends to the international community of Islamic nations in the political arena.

It's not that I find Muslims much worse than Christians in their behavior. My problem is their extravagant claims to a unified Islam in which all are equal. Islam seeks to present the unity of worshipers performing the Hajj as a norm, whereas it is anomalous to reality.

Another prohibition of the Hajj relates to marital relationships.

Narrated Abu Huraira: The Prophet said, "Whoever performs Hajj for Allah's pleasure and does not have sexual relations with his wife, and does not do evil or sins, then he will return (after Hajj free from all sins) as if he were born anew" (2:347–48; 26.4.596).

Sexual activity, in Islam, has a negative effect on religious rituals such as the Ramadan fast and the Hajj. It is not that sex is bad. However, it is a regulated activity that is to be set aside during a time of intense spiritual quest. Few references are found in the Hadith to "born-again" Muslims. In this passage we see the formula for such an experience. The Hajj has a cleansing effect on the pilgrim and brings him to the position of an innocent newborn infant. This is to be understood in light of Islam's not holding to the doctrine of original sin; thus, the new status is one of purity and innocence.

Aisha sets forth another criterion for ceremonial cleanness.

Narrated Aisha: I was menstruating when I reached Mecca. So, I neither performed Tawaf [circumambulation] of the Kaaba, nor the Tawaf between Safa and Marwa. Then I informed Allah's apostle about it. He replied, "Perform all the ceremonies of Hajj like the other pilgrims, but do not perform the Tawaf of the Kaaba until you get clean (from your menses)" (2:416; 26.80.172).

Menstruation negates the effect of prayers, fasting, and portions of the Hajj. The Muslim woman is to temporarily abstain from these rituals until her period is completed. Then she is to continue in her religious obligations.

It can be said the Hajj is the largest regular concentration of religious pilgrims in the world. For the Hajji it is the absolute apex of religious experience. But has the Muslim really thought through

the apparent contradiction of orthodox Islamic theology compared to a ritual so animistic in form, if not in content? Kissing
a holy stone seems incompatible with the pure worship of a God
who is spirit. Islam's denunciations of idolatry contrasts with the
prescribed rituals of the Hajj. These facts can be carefully shared
with Muslims.

lmsgiving

uch of the Muslim world is extremely poor. Still, it is incumbent on all adherents to give 2.5 percent of their income to the needy. This is not only an obligatory teaching, but is also one of the five foundational pillars of Islam.

It is my observation that soliciting rather than giving best represents the day-by-day practice of many Muslim people. Some analysts attribute this to the subservience experienced while Muslims lived under the extended colonial rule of the West. Others point to ongoing poverty in much of the Islamic world as the key cause for what appears to be nothing less than a begging mentality and lifestyle. A few critics would contend that a religion of works that rewards the giving of alms will invariably create a significant body of beggars.

I have found it painful to live for many years among a segment of Muslims who have lost their personal dignity and self-respect and, by and large, do not even know it. Repetitious pleading for assistance on a personal and national level has, almost unconsciously, become an acceptable way of life.

Reasons for Almsgiving

In light of Quranic and Hadith teaching on assisting the needy, my very being cries out in protest against some extremely wealthy

oil-producing countries doing so little for their suffering brothers in the faith. A country like Bangladesh pays top dollar for
imported oil from Middle Eastern Islamic countries. Some Two-
Thirds World Muslim nations are forced to turn obsequiously to
the West for food and development assistance. An indication of
the Prophet's view on this subject is the following Hadith.

> Narrated Abu Huraira: The Prophet said, "No doubt, it is better
> for a person to take a rope and proceed in the morning to the
> mountains and cut the wood and then sell it, and eat from this
> income and give alms from it than to ask others for something"
> (2:325; 24.52.558).

Here is a straightforward teaching that exalts the dignity of labor
in contrast to the demeaning expediency of begging. The worker
is told to give alms to the less fortunate. An obvious complication
is a society in which many are motivated to work but employment
opportunities are minimal. I have met Muslim college graduates
who have been forced to work in menial employment. Their
willingness to do so is commendable.

Another Tradition parallels a biblical model.

> Narrated Abu Huraira: The Prophet said, "A person who gives in
> charity so secretly that his left hand does not know what his right
> hand has given (then he will be under the shade of Allah's Throne
> on the Day of Resurrection)" (2:287; 24.12.501).

In the mosque there is usually a large steel box to be found near
the door. This is the *zakat* or offering box. On their way out of the
mosque Muslims slip their gift unpretentiously into the slit in the
top cover. I have never seen an offering plate passed during a time
of worship in the mosque. I doubt that it is done.

The mosque committee members also solicit donations from
the Muslim community. This may be done in order to pay the
imam, meet upkeep expenses, or assist in building costs. This
solicitation can be done rather vigorously. Cars and busses have
been stopped forcibly while donations were sought.

In contrast to the anonymity commended in the Hadith, I have
seen large blackboards placed outside of mosques. Written in
large letters were the names and donations given by those who

attended that particular mosque. Part of the motivation to give seemed to center on the publicity that would follow.

Apart from giving to the mosque, it is mandatory for Muslims to care for the needs of their relatives.

> The Prophet said, "The one who gives Zakat to his family shall get double reward; one for fulfilling the rights of his family, and the other for paying the Zakat" (2:312; 24.43.539).

I was a bit taken aback when I first learned that Muslims regularly give their religious offerings to their parents. This Hadith even gives double merit for such an act. In the Christian tradition we would regard financial obligations to parents as a personal expense quite apart from our gifts to Christian ministries. Islam is more integrated in its world view, seeing religion as permeating all relationships. "Honor thy father and mother" is as much a command in Islam as it is in Judaism and Christianity. In some Muslim countries, all official papers designate a man as "the son of. . . ." His identity is one with his family. Therefore he feels it is only right for religious offerings to be given to parents as a fulfillment of his familial obligation. My observation is that such assistance is given with joy and out of a deep sense of gratitude for all one has received from one's parents.

Muhammad considered it proper to command women to give alms.

> Narrated Abdur-Rahman bin Abis: Then the Prophet ordered (the women) to give alms, and they started stretching out their hands towards their ears and throats (giving their ornaments in charity), and the Prophet ordered Bilal to go to them (to collect the alms), and then Bilal returned to the Prophet (9:318; 92.16.426).

Warnings Against Withholding Alms

Islam clearly presents the antithesis between God's blessings and God's judgments. Obedience is rewarded. Disobedience is penalized. This holds true in regard to sharing one's resources with God and others.

Narrated Asma bint Abu Bakr: The Prophet said, "Do not shut your money bag; otherwise Allah too will withhold His blessings from you. Spend (in Allah's Cause) as much as you can afford" (2:295; 24.21.515).

Withheld blessings are to be interpreted much as Christians would view the subject. To the Muslim, illness, loss of employment, financial difficulty, emotional trauma, and accidents all find their first cause in Allah's sovereign work in one's life. To refuse to contribute money in God's name will bring these or other misfortunes.

The fires of hell are said to await the recalcitrant giver.

Narrated Adi bin Hatim: Allah's Apostle said, "Each one of you will stand in front of Allah and there will be neither a curtain nor an interpreter between him and Allah, and Allah will ask him, 'Did not I give you wealth?' He will reply in the affirmative. Allah will further ask, 'Didn't I send a messenger (or Prophet) to you?' And again that person will reply in the affirmative. Then he will look to his right and he will see nothing but Hell-fire, and then he will look to his left and will see nothing but Hell-fire. And so, any (each one) of you should save himself from the Hell-fire even by giving half of a date-fruit (in charity). And if you do not find a half date-fruit, then (you can do it through saying) a good pleasant word (to your brethren)" (2:283; 24.8.494).

As the case is presented here, the Muslim can avoid hell with relative ease. In the time of Muhammad, dates were a cheap and readily available fruit. If giving half a date proved problematic, then all that was required was for the Muslim to say a kind word to a fellow believer.

Other Traditions, however, have a harsher tone:

Narrated Abu Dhar: The Prophet said "Whoever had camels or cows or sheep and did not pay their Zakat [offering], those animals will be brought on the Day of Resurrection far bigger and fatter than before and they will tread him under their hooves, and will butt him with their horns, and (those animals will come in circle): When the last does its turn, the first will start again, and this punishment will go on until Allah has finished His judgements among the people" (2:311; 24.42.539).

Being trod under the hooves of camels for an extended period would seemingly be a powerful motivator for becoming a generous benefactor. Even more graphic is this Hadith, which depicts a snake as God's instrument of judgment.

> Narrated Abu Huraira: Allah's Apostle said, "Whoever is made wealthy by Allah and does not pay the Zakat of his wealth, then on the Day of Resurrection his wealth will be made like a bald-headed poisonous male snake with two black spots over the eyes. The snake will encircle his neck and bite his cheeks and say, 'I am your wealth, I am your treasure'" (2:276–77; 24.2.486).

Islam does not teach that having riches is inherently wrong. A question can be raised as to whether Islam condones a particular economic system for its followers. One could say communism promotes equal distribution of resources for all; capitalism espouses free enterprise with personal initiative receiving the greatest reward; and socialism allows for state as well as private ownership. Socialism seeks to provide for the poor by a system of welfare benefits. At the same time it allows for the highly motivated to attain great riches.

Islam promotes itself as a theocracy. God is the ruler of his kingdom of followers. The Quran and Hadith reveal Allah's will in all areas, thus making Islam a total code of life. But how can this work out economically for the worldwide community of Islam? There is no dogmatic answer to this question, but one can make a few observations about the practical dimension of finances in many Islamic countries:

1. Most Muslims are deprived and needy.
2. Socialism, with a bias toward capitalism, has prevailed in a significant number of nations in which Muslims are a majority. This has helped create a small wealthy elite class who rule the country. The middle class is almost nonexistent, while the great mass of citizens is extremely poor. Health care is theoretically provided free for all needy people. In practice, this socialized medicine is a massive failure. There is a shortage of hospitals, doctors, nurses, and medicine in most rural areas of Muslim countries.

3. Islam clearly teaches against charging or receiving interest among fellow Muslims. This is an Old Testament command for Jews as well. This prohibition is seldom followed in Islam, either on a national or an individual level. This is a definite problem to Muslim theologians.
4. Zakat, in a few countries, is collected by the government. This is resented by many, especially by nominal Muslims.

In the context of such widespread poverty one can at least understand why almsgiving is more an ideal than a reality. What often happens is that an extended family makes every effort to provide adequately for the needs of its own sociological unit. Beyond that, few venture to go.

I leave the angels to have the last word on the subject.

Narrated Abu Huraira: The Prophet said, "Every day two angels come down from Heaven and one of them says, 'O Allah! Compensate every person who spends in Your cause,' and the other (angel) says, 'O Allah! Destroy every miser'" (2:299; 24.26.522).

Jihad and Violence

J ane Wells, a friend in America, wrote to me,

> When I taught preschool five years ago, we had children from all over the world. Among our seventy-five kids, I once counted eleven languages! But I remember a little Filipino boy who was so thoroughly Muslim and so violent in his speaking and thinking that it chilled me—this in a four-year-old! He had some sort of stick weapon with which he "charged" in the name of Allah. I tried to tell him that Allah would not want him to hurt anyone.

Is this behavior a norm or an anomaly? This chapter seeks to explore the issue.

Jihad (holy war) is and always has been a powerful force in Islam. It is one of the few Arabic words known by educated people the world over. Television and print media have brought the reality of this term into the living rooms of millions of homes. To the non-Muslim it is a word of horror associated most closely with Arab terrorists. Mental pictures of hijacked planes and blown-up military barracks are integrally connected with jihad.

Muslims are somewhat ambivalent with this concept that causes them both pride and shame. Pride because of the close association jihad has with the will of Allah. A holy war is said to bear the sanction of God himself. Jihad is launched against those who are the enemies of truth and all that is right and ultimate. Shame because of hermeneutical difficulties. When Iran and Iraq squared off against each other and both declared jihad, who really was on the side of Allah? Palestinian jihadists may have a legitimate cause, but can it possibly include the indiscriminate killing of women and children who happen to be in an inopportune place when an operation is executed?

Gentle Muslims are prone to emphasize that the "greater jihad" refers to a spiritual warfare against sin and all that is antithetical to Allah. Greater jihad is an internal battle for righteousness that should take place in the life of every Muslim. There can be no argument against such a jihad. But the "lesser jihad," which refers to the traditional interpretation of holy war, is still a reality that continues to have a high profile worldwide.

It needs to be noted that Islam does not stand alone in regard to the embarrassment flowing from the activities of religious zealots. The Christian Crusades from the eleventh to the fourteenth centuries may be but a small footnote in our history textbooks, but to Muslims those years of brutality are a pungent memory of a historical violation against their ancestors. Other religious traditions can be indicted for jihadic activity as well.

As will be seen in this chapter, the Hadith gives powerful authentication for violence utilized against "infidels" or those who, having once converted to Islam, renounce the faith and return to their former state. The brutality of these passages is overwhelming. It is from these early teachings and acts of the Prophet that we see contemporary Muslims feeling justified in their acts of aggression. Many incidents that have been termed jihad by modern Muslims would most likely not be acceptable to Muhammad. There is no record of his assent to the killing of innocent children in blatant acts of politically motivated terrorism.

So, my emotions recoil in horror as I interact with the violent intimidation found in the teaching and precedents set forth in the Hadith. But I must be fair. My mind and heart equally struggle with the Joshua accounts of God-mandated destruction of men, women, children, and animals. The imprecatory Psalms, which rail against one's enemies, cause me to shudder, as does the desire of the psalmist to see the infants of Babylon dashed against the rocks (Ps. 137). Everything in me desires to speed forward to Jesus and his teaching that commands me to love my enemies and turn my cheek to the persecutor. I await a day of fuller understanding God's perspective. In the meantime, my small mind struggles with concepts of consistency and integrity.

The Purposes of Jihad

The importance of jihad is clearly set out by Muhammad.

> Narrated Abdullah: I asked the Prophet, "Which deed is the dearest to Allah?" He replied, "To offer prayers at their fixed times." I asked, "What is the next (in goodness)?" He replied, "To be good and dutiful to your parents." I again asked: "What is the next (in goodness)?" He replied, "To participate in Jihad (religious fighting) in Allah's cause" (1:300; 10.5.505).

Here we have a prioritization of the concerns of Allah: prayer, parents, and jihad. All three receive considerable emphasis in the Quran, Hadith, and in the teaching of Islamic teachers down through the centuries.

It is important to put the original teaching of jihad in historical perspective. Muhammad was locked in a battle with idolaters for his very survival. He was convinced he was the conduit for Allah's revelation. This truth was not just for Arabs; rather it was a universal path of salvation for all people of all ages. Apparently Muhammad was obsessed with the responsibility to propagate this message. Therefore, it seemed logical to him to utilize force against any obstacle that stood in the way of God's truth. In this manner, Islam spread in its early days: first, proclamation, and if that failed, coercive methods.

Unfortunately for the non-Muslim world, there are today followers of Islam who feel totally justified in applying violent means to achieve an end that they are convinced is in harmony with God's will. The Ayatollah Khomeini simply could not countenance a reprobate Muslim having the audacity to slander the Prophet. Jihad was declared and millions of dollars offered to the Muslim who will find a way to assassinate Salman Rushdie. In less dramatic situations, both nations and individuals have experienced the wrath of Muslims who have outworked jihad in a manner they felt conformed to the will of God.

Muhammad's deep commitment to "Allah's cause," unadulterated with selfish motivation, is presented in this Hadith.

> Narrated Abu Musa: A man came to the Prophet and asked, "A man fights for war booty; another fights for fame and a third fights for showing off; which of them fights in Allah's Cause?" The Prophet said, "He who fights so that Allah's Word (i.e. Islam) should be superior, fights in Allah's Cause" (4:50; 52.15.65).

A further tradition states unequivocally that Muhammad is ordered by God to force the conversion of nonbelievers to Islam.

> Narrated Abu Huraira: Allah's Apostle said, "I have been ordered (by Allah) to fight the people till they say: 'None has the right to be worshipped but Allah,' and whoever said it then he will save his life and property. . . ." (2:274; 24.1.483).

A missionary wife, kidnaped by Muslim terrorists, was released after the host government paid a ransom. At one point in her nine-day captivity, the Muslims threw her Bible into the shrubs and said, "If you become a Muslim, we will release you." It would appear these men had been reading Al-Bukhari! The way to save one's life and property is to become a Muslim. I must say I find this teaching to be repugnant. Christians have been accused by Muslims of inducing conversion. But I am not aware of any situation in this century in which a Muslim has been pressed to convert to Christ or lose his or her life and property.

A further Hadith has Muhammad demanding land from Jews.

> Narrated Abu Huraira: While we were in the mosque, Allah's Apostle came out and said, "Let us proceed to the Jews." So we went out with him till we came to Bait-al-Midras. The Prophet stood up there and called them, saying, "O assembly of Jews! Surrender to Allah (embrace Islam) and you will be safe!" They said, "You have conveyed Allah's message, O Aba-al-Qasim." Allah's Apostle then said to them, "That is what I want; embrace Islam and you will be safe." They said, "You have conveyed the message, O Aba-al-Qasim." Allah's Apostle then said to them, "That is what I want," and repeated his words for the third time and added, "Know that

the earth is for Allah and I want to exile you from this land, so whoever among you has property he should sell it, otherwise, know that the land is for Allah and His Apostle" (9:327; 92.18.447).

A number of Traditions touch on ownership of land. If all property truly belongs to Allah, then, Muslims reason, it is only right to seek to consolidate the land of the earth under the banner and control of Islam. This would appear to be the driving force behind the early jihadic crusades across the Middle East and North Africa. Although Muslims justifiably resent the colonial domination of their countries in the nineteenth and twentieth centuries, the question can be posed as to whether they were any more morally correct in their many imperialistic forays.

Allah was said to be protective of his anointed Prophet.

Narrated Ibn Abbas: Allah's Wrath became severe on him whom the Prophet had killed in Allah's Cause. Allah's Wrath became severe on the people who caused the face of Allah's Prophet to bleed (5:277; 59.23.401).

The followers of Muhammad were highly motivated to wage battle against nonbelievers.

Narrated Hisham: My father informed me that Aisha said, "Sa'd said, 'O Allah! You know that there is nothing more beloved to me than to fight in Your Cause against those who disbelieved Your Apostle and turned him out (of Mecca)'" (5:309; 59.29.448).

As I read these words of emotional intensity, I cringe at the devastating potential of religious fervor. Fighting and killing is depicted as a beloved activity. How can God's will become so grotesquely distorted? In 1212, during the Crusades, hundreds of boys and girls, mostly under the age of twelve, left the shores of France absolutely convinced they were being obedient to God. With the blessing of the church they set their sights on driving the "infidel Muslims" from the Holy Land. Not one of these children reached Jerusalem. Almost all died of hunger or shipwreck. The rest were sold into slavery to Muslims when they reached Islamic strongholds. These precious children, and their parents, were unquestionably sincere. But their misguided zeal led them on to destruction much as that experienced by Muslim Iranian teenagers who, in the name of Allah, walked into the minefields separating Iran and Iraq during their war in the 1980s. This type of fanaticism provides great fuel for the attacks of sneering agnostics against any and all forms of organized religion. I can at least understand their attitude.

There was an age limit of fifteen before young men were allowed to enter battle.

> Narrated Ibn Umar that the Prophet inspected him on the day of Uhud while he was fourteen years old, and the Prophet did not allow him to take part in the battle. He was inspected again by the Prophet on the day of Al-Khandaq (i.e. battle of the Trench) while he was fifteen years old, and the Prophet allowed him to take part in the battle (5:294; 59.28.423).

Violence as an Expression of Jihad

> Narrated Anas: Whenever Allah's Apostle attacked some people, he would never attack them till it was dawn. If he heard the Adhan (i.e., call for prayer) he would delay the fight, and if he did not hear the Adhan, he would attack them immediately after dawn (4:123; 52.102.193).

There was a total integration between spiritual exercises and jihad. The concept of Allah was ethereally bathed in pragmatic violence. At all costs, the Islamic kingdom was to be extended, first in Arabia, then the Middle East, North Africa, and the whole world. The end seemingly justified the means.

Muslim scholars regularly seek to downplay the force that was threatened or used in the early days of the spread of Islam. They emphasize the weakness of the extensive Byzantine Empire. These historians, working within their own biases, declare that millions were waiting for a religious alternative. When Muslim warriors appeared, the people were said to be only too glad to convert, both religiously and politically. Certain Hadith give other indications:

> Narrated Jubair bin Haiya: Umar sent the Muslims to the great countries to fight the pagans. . . .

. . . [The people under siege asked the Muslims who they are]
Al-Mughira replied, "We are some people from the Arabs; we led
a hard, miserable, disastrous life; we used to suck the hides and
the date stones from hunger; we used to wear clothes made up of
fur of camels and hair of goats, and to worship trees and stones.
While we were in this state, the Lord of the Heavens and the Earths,
Elevated is His Remembrance and Majestic is His Highness, sent
to us from among ourselves a Prophet whose father and mother
are known to us. Our Prophet, the Messenger of our Lord, has
ordered us to fight you until you worship Allah Alone or give Jizya
(i.e. tribute)" (4:254–55; 53.21.386).

So the colonized were given a choice: Convert . . . or pay a
tax, thus becoming a second-class citizen and thereby able to
retain one's own religious belief. Not much of a choice for poor
people whose country has just been conquered by a powerful
alien force. In most instances their prior religious commitment
was superficial, thus making the option of becoming Muslims
compelling. The Christian Copts of Egypt were a tenacious community who refused to convert. They were the exception rather
than the rule.

Now, compare this with the motivation and methodology of
Western colonizers in the last two centuries. Their motivation
was greed, not religion. Their methodology was the carrot and
the stick. "Divide and conquer" was the tool of choice in political domination. Force was to be used only in the last instance.
Religious sentiments of the colonized were to be respected. It is
true that Christian missionaries followed on the heels of the soldiers, but their methods were proclamation and social uplift.
Jihadic activity simply was not utilized.

One can then ask why Muslims get so irritated concerning
Christian missionary activity. We cannot compare with Islam in
the use of violence in propagation methodology. The answer lies
in Islam's absolute conviction that it possesses ultimate truth and
therefore must actively oppose all intrusion into its religious
domain. Just five days prior to the writing of these words, Muslims in my country of residence shot an Italian Roman Catholic
priest. Some days prior to his murder he had been sent a grenade
by mail with a note telling him to immediately desist from seek-

ing to convert Muslims to Christianity. He paid the ultimate price
for invading Islam's territory.

In one instance Muhammad "invoked evil" on those who dis-
agreed with his religious convictions:

> Narrated Masruq: The Quraish delayed in embracing Islam for a
> period, so the Prophet invoked evil on them, saying, "O Allah!
> Help me against them by sending seven years of (famine) like those
> of Joseph." So they were afflicted with such a severe year of famine
> that they were destroyed therein and ate dead animals and bones.
> They started seeing something like smoke between the sky and the
> earth (because of severe hunger) (6:282–83; 60.229.297).

All of this occurred because of a refusal by the Quraish to accept
an opposing view of God. Perhaps the Prophet could have used
his power in prayer in a more benign manner by asking Allah to
reveal his truth to the skeptics through dreams or visions. Why
purposefully torment detractors into acquiescence?

> Narrated Qais: When Jarir reached Yemen, there was a man who
> used to foretell and give good omens by casting arrows of divina-
> tion. Someone said to him, "The messenger of Allah's Apostle is
> present here and if he should get hold of you, he would chop off
> your neck." One day while he was using them (i.e. arrows of div-
> ination), Jarir stopped there and said to him, "Break them (i.e. the
> arrows) and testify that none has the right to be worshiped except
> Allah, or else I will chop off your neck." So the man broke those
> arrows and testified that none has the right to be worshiped except
> Allah (5:452; 59.61.643).

Following in the footsteps of the Prophet, Jarir confronts a
practitioner of divination and threatens to behead him unless he
makes a profession of Islamic faith. The man's use of the arrows
was limited to foretelling the future or giving good omens. His
activities, although I do not agree with them, were still benign.
Why was he threatened with a violent death?

In another incident, Muhammad sends out his executioners.

> Narrated Al-Bara: Allah's Apostle sent Abdullah bin Atik and
> Abdullah bin Utba with a group of men to Abu Rafi (to kill him).
> . . . [Abdullah said,] "I saw the house in complete darkness with

its lights off, and I could not know where the man was. So I called, 'O Abu Rafi!' He replied, 'Who is it?' I proceeded towards the voice and hit him. He cried loudly but my blow was futile. Then I came to him, pretending to help him, saying with a different tone of my voice, 'What is wrong with you, O Abu Rafi?' He said, 'Are you not surprised? Woe on your mother! A man has come to me and hit me with a sword!' So again I aimed at him and hit him, but the blow proved futile again, and on that Abu Rafi cried loudly and his wife got up. I came again and changed my voice as if I were a helper, and found Abu Rafi lying straight on his back, so I drove the sword into his belly and bent on it till I heard the sound of a bone break. Then I came out, filled with astonishment, and went to the staircase to descend, but I fell down from it and got my leg dislocated. I bandaged it and went to my companions limping. I said (to them), 'Go and tell Allah's Apostle of this good news, but I will not leave (this place) till I hear the news of his (i.e. Abu Rafi's) death.' When dawn broke, an announcer of death got over the wall and announced, 'I convey to you the news of Abu Rafi's death.' I got up and proceeded without feeling any pain till I caught up with my companions before they reached the Prophet to whom I conveyed the good news" (5:253–55; 59.15.372).

It almost seems there is delight in giving the gory details of this murder. Why would the Hadith present such a vivid and gruesome account? A killing can be chronicled without such specifics. Is there some psychotic phenomenon operational within the concept of jihad?

> Narrated Abdullah: The Prophet recited Surat-an-Najm [a chapter of the Quran] at Mecca and prostrated while reciting it and those who were with him did the same except an old man who took a handful of small stones or earth and lifted it to his forehead and said, "This is sufficient for me." Later on, I saw him killed as a non-believer (2:100; 19.1.173).

Was this old man a threat to anyone? He did not seem willing to follow the Islamic practices of Muhammad, but it is hard to see anything in his behavior that would be worthy of death. This passage declares he was killed solely because of his refusal to convert to Islam.

Narrated Aisha: [Gabriel said:] "Go out to them (to attack them)."
The Prophet said, "Where?" Gabriel pointed towards Bani
Quraiza. So Allah's Apostle went to them (i.e. Bani Quraiza) (i.e.
besieged them). They then surrendered to the Prophet's judgement
but he directed them to Sa'd to give his verdict concerning them.
Sa'd said, "I give my judgment that their warriors should be killed,
their women and children should be taken as captives, and their
properties distributed" (5:309; 59.29.448).

In this Hadith we have Gabriel, an angel, ordering Muhammad into battle. We then have a pathetic picture of a defeated
enemy surrendering to the Prophet and most likely begging for
mercy. Sa'd was directed to give final judgment as to their fate.
The context indicates Muhammad agreed with Sa'd's decision.
The soldiers were to be executed while the women and children
became slaves (and concubines) of the Islamic victors. Land was
to be given to the Muslim conquerors. This was standard procedure for Muslims and non-Muslims alike. My problem relates to
an angel and a Prophet of God in the seventh century A.D. having such an integral part in the murder of surrendered soldiers
and the enslavement of women and children, whose only sin was
probably that of biological linkage to Muhammad's enemies.
However one may desire to minimize the severity of these acts
by referring to historical context, I still find it reprehensible.

Narrated Abu Huraira: Allah's Apostle said, "The Hour will not
be established until you fight with the Jews, and the stone behind
which a Jew will be hiding says, 'O Muslim! There is a Jew hiding
behind me, so kill him'" (4:110; 52.94.177).

It is fairly easy to document the Muslim's inbuilt hatred against
the Jews as we investigate the Quran and Hadith. Jews refused to
accept Muhammad as a unique prophet of God. For this denial,
they became an object of Muhammad's wrath. This antagonism
sparked the takeover of Palestine very shortly after the Prophet's
death. Such high-level animosity has never been resolved down
through the centuries. In recent decades it has been further complicated by conflicting claims and terroristic activities throughout the Middle East.

In the preceding Hadith we see the Prophet foretelling a day in which an inert stone becomes an animated coconspirator against Jews. Even a rock will condemn the Jew to death. Some will respond that this Hadith is not to be taken literally, but allegories carry a powerful message.

The issue of forsaking Islam in favor of another religion or ideology is dealt with in this Tradition.

> Narrated Ikrima: The statement of Allah's Apostle, "Whoever changed his Islamic religion, then kill him" (9:45; 84.2.57).

This penalty is reinforced in a further Hadith.

> Narrated Abu Musa: A man embraced Islam and then reverted back to Judaism. Muadh bin Jabal came and saw the man with Abu Musa. Muadh asked, "What is wrong with this (man)?" Abu Musa replied, "He embraced Islam and then reverted back to Judaism." Muadh said, "I will not sit down unless you kill him (as it is) the verdict of Allah and His Apostle (9:201; 89.12.271).

The law of apostasy is thus spelled out with unmistakable clarity. Conversion to Islam is not only encouraged but at times has been forcibly induced. Conversion from Islam is punishable by instant death. It doesn't always work this way. Many Muslims have come to Christ in countries like Indonesia with few if any repercussions. In other fundamentalist Islamic states, however, a significant number of Muslim converts have paid for their faith in Christ with their lives. The executioners plead the protection of Islamic theology. It is, they say, a command of Allah himself to not allow any Muslim to deny the true faith of Islam. Freedom of religion, to many followers of Islam, is interpreted to mean everyone has the right to practice his or her own faith. Beyond that, any non-Muslim can accept Islam as the true path. But at that point the "freedom" ceases. Muslims come under the penalty of death in certain countries if they renounce Islam in favor of any religious alternative.

Interestingly, in those same nations, the Muslim can safely lapse into worldliness. He can cease praying and attending the mosque. Even the Ramadan fast may be violated in the privacy of his own home. But the moment this same Muslim publicly renounces faith in Islam and the Prophet, he is vulnerable to the sentence of death. This seems to be a coercive intimidation unworthy of the claim of God's imprimatur.

Although the worldly Muslim in contemporary society survives, this does not mean the Prophet condones such activity. This Tradition gives a direct warning to the hypocrite.

> Narrated Ali: I heard the Prophet saying, "In the last days (of the world) there will appear young people with foolish thoughts and ideas. They will give good talks, but they will go out of Islam as an arrow goes out of its game, their faith will not exceed their throats. So, wherever you find them, kill them, for there will be a reward for their killers on the Day of Resurrection" (6:519; 61.36.577).

I am not sure whether we are living in the "last days" according to Islamic belief, but I am convinced that hundreds of thousands of Muslim young men would be killed if we are! As I mix with Muslim youth four afternoons a week, I am convinced few are following the dictates of Islam. Should they be killed for their youthful waywardness? This Hadith proclaims the executioners as heroes who will be rewarded on the day of resurrection.

Rewards for Jihad

Various types and degrees of rewards are presented in the Hadith for those who assist in the punishment of the non-Muslim.

> Narrated Abu Qatada: Allah's Apostle said, "Whoever had killed an infidel and has a proof or a witness for it, then the salb (arms and belongings of that deceased) will be for him" (9:213; 89.21.282).

These words seem mercenary. Certainly, motivation could become confusing. Do you kill because of Islam or to obtain a new weapon? Does killing become dependent on the relative wealth of potential victims? The richer the infidel, the greater the reward for his dispatch into eternity. This is foreign to the concept of a loving and merciful God. It rather portrays a crude doctrine of the survival of the fittest.

Narrated Khalid bin Madan: The Prophet said, "The first army amongst my followers who will invade Caesar's City will be forgiven their sins" (4:109; 52.93.175).

Muhammad had a vision for making Islam a universal religion. One of the keys to fulfilling this desire would be to conquer Rome in the name of Allah. One could question what right Muhammad's armies would have to invade a powerful city and impose their religion on its inhabitants. The answer is that it is the will of Allah for all heathen everywhere to become Muslims.

In this Tradition Muhammad gives assurance of warriors having their sins forgiven because of their involvement in jihad. This promise seemed to apply only to the first army to enter Rome. Most likely this was because of the inevitably high casualty rate of the initial wave of soldiers seeking to penetrate the city. In fourteen hundred years of history, this particular promise of forgiven sins is yet to be claimed by Muslim warriors. Rome remains unconquered by Islam.

Narrated Abu Huraira: Allah's Apostle said, "Five are regarded as martyrs: They are those who die because of plague, abdominal disease, drowning or a falling building etc., and the martyrs in Allah's Cause" (4:62; 52.30.82).

These words of Muhammad seem strange. Why would a Muslim be declared a martyr because he or she died of disease or an accident? More to the point, a Muslim who is killed in jihad is to be honored as a martyr. This belief is very strong in Islam. It has emboldened many to willingly lay down their lives on the battlefield. Martyrdom bestows an honorable name to the family that is left behind. It also guarantees entry into paradise for the martyr.

Narrated Abu Huraira: Allah's Apostle said, "To the person who carries out Jihad for His Cause and nothing compelled him to go out but the Jihad in His Cause, and belief in His Words, Allah guarantees that He will either admit him into Paradise or return him with the reward or the booty he has earned to his residence from where he went out" (9:413; 93.28.549).

Muhammad links jihad very closely with God's cause and God's Word. One can never begin to fathom the compelling power of jihad until the intimate linkage of Allah and the holy war is comprehended. It is not man's dictates that promote violence. Allah is the first cause and supreme commander of all jihadic activity. That being a given, there can be no reluctance or guilt associated with involvement in jihad.

What a bountiful guarantee is given by Allah to participants in his holy war. If they die, they go immediately to paradise and if they survive, they will return home with abundant booty.

> Narrated Jabir bin Abdullah: On the day of the battle of Uhud, a man came to the Prophet and said, "Can you tell me where I will be if I should get martyred?" The Prophet replied, "In Paradise." The man threw away some dates he was carrying in his hand, and fought till he was martyred (5:260; 59.16.377).

This anonymous follower of Islam was given a powerful word of assurance of paradise by the Prophet. This motivation emboldened the soldier to enter the battle with such great zeal that he was soon martyred. Would the man have been willing to fight unto death if the Prophet had not bestowed the promise of paradise upon him?

Religious fervor can be devastating. In one Southeast Asian country a Muslim young woman became a convinced follower of Christ. She became the object of intense persecution from her family. Her attention was drawn to the biblical assurance of eternal life with all the exciting promises of the Book of Revelation. All of this seemed to be in marked contrast with her present life, which was filled with physical and emotional pain. One memorable and sad day, this woman committed suicide.

The presentation of religion carries with it an awesome responsibility. Balance and perspective must be presented accurately. Promises of eternal life must never be the motivation of suicide or jihad unto death.

> Narrated Abu Huraira: Allah's Apostle said, "None is wounded in Allah's Cause but will come on the Day of Resurrection with his wound bleeding. The thing that will come out of his wound will be the color of blood, but its smell will be the smell of musk" (7:314–15; 67.31.441).

Muhammad down plays the injuries sustained while engaged in jihad. All will be made right on the day of resurrection.

Reflection

This has not been an easy chapter for me to write. I have never written so extensively on Islamic jihad. Two factors have compelled me to write as I have. The first reason is obvious. Islamic belief and practice as stated in the Hadith undeniably affirm religious violence. Secondly, on a much more personal basis, I simply deplore warfare of any nature, be it personal or national, religious or nonreligious.

A question could then be raised concerning my presuppositions. Am I a pacifist? I struggle to give an answer. My early manhood was spent between wars, so I never had to face the draft. But of this I am confident, I could never willfully kill another person. But this does not exclude the possibility and even probability that I would have been willing to serve in the armed forces as a chaplain.

The exegesis of this conviction comes from two sources. First of all, I see the New Testament exhorting us to give our enemies love rather than death. Second, the sensitive side of my nature cannot bear to see people suffer. These statements then bring us to the concept of a "just war." What about the systematic genocide of six million Jews under the horrific pogrom of Adolph Hitler? If no action had been taken by Allied forces, there may not have been one Jew alive today. A few years ago my wife and I relived that historical moment by walking the streets of Auschwitz. If good force is not utilized to overcome evil, then we are left with chaos and destruction. Is that the will of God?

There are no easy ideological or religious answers to this complex problem. But can we not at least make a few observations? Would not a "demonstration" nuclear bombing of an isolated island near Tokyo have sufficed? Could the United States forces not have pulled out of Vietnam much earlier? Are there not creative alternatives to the use of the devastating armaments that are held by so many countries today? Who can applaud warfare when it invariably results in the killing and maiming of countless innocent people?

So, with that background, I must go on to say that I cannot indulge the thought of religious jihad . . . by anyone. Admittedly, I struggle the most with Old Testament passages. But in contemporary society how can the clarion call of jihad be used to mobilize force against those who do not agree with one's particular religious conviction?

Let "lesser jihad" be forever renounced by all religious forces: Shiites against Sunnis, Iranian Muslims against Bahais, Egyptian Muslims against Christian Copts, Indian Hindus against Muslims, Bangladeshi Muslims against Hindus, Irish Protestants against Roman Catholics, or in any conflict in which God is given as the *raison d'etre* for violent aggression.

In regard to jihad, we as followers of Christ are in a favorable position to allow our New Testament to be compared with the Quran and the Hadith. Why has Islam, revealed six hundred years after our Testament of love and forgiveness, reverted two thousand years to an Old Covenant world view of aggression and retribution? We could wish Muslim scholars would seek to better understand historical and contemporary jihad. They could be the key to issuing proclamations that could lead to denouncing the terrible deeds of violence done in Allah's name by Muslims.

Punishments for Sin

Many of the moral perspectives of the Judeo-Christian tradition have been incorporated into Islamic theology and practice. Adultery, lying, cheating, stealing, and hate are all condemned in the three great monotheistic religions. Islam, however, does bring a number of unique ethical distinctives to the religious scene. Some of these will be explored in this chapter.

One passage gives an overview of what the Prophet considered important in the area of morals. It starts with a strong theological affirmation and then moves on to practical ethics. Punishment for sin in this life is presented as an expiation and a cleansing. The ultimate judge of all sin is Allah, who may or may not exercise mercy toward the sinner.

Narrated Ubada bin As-Samit: I, along with a group of people, gave the pledge of allegiance to Allah's Apostle. He said, "I take your Pledge on the condition that you (1) will not join partners in worship with Allah, (2) will not steal, (3) will not commit illegal sexual intercourse, (4) will not kill your offspring, (5) will not slander, (6) and will not disobey me when I order you to do good. Whoever among you will abide by his pledge, his reward will be with

Allah, and whoever commits any of those sins and receives the punishment in this world, that punishment will be an expiation for his sins and purification; but if Allah screens him, then it will be up to Allah to punish him if He will or excuse him if He will" (9:420; 93.31.560).

Humiliation for Pride

Narrated Jundub: The Prophet said, "He who does good things in public to show off and win the praise of the people, Allah will disclose his real intention (and humiliate him)" (8:334; 76.36.506).

Pride and hypocrisy are powerful deterrents to genuine spirituality. Islam recognizes this fact and its Scriptures repeatedly denounce these two sins. In this Hadith the Prophet gives assurance that humiliation from Allah awaits the proud and hypocritical sinner. The teaching is that if the unrighteous person will not humble himself, then God will perform the task for him.

It is common to accuse Muslims of arrogance. "Ours is the best community." "Islam is the only path to God." "Allah favors only Muslims with blessings." Such statements are commonly expressed by followers of the Prophet. I admit to being frustrated as, over the years, I have had to confront absolute dogmatism on the part of so many Muslim acquaintances. In multiple instances, there seems to be no critical facility with which to interact with the heavy and obscure issues of life. Rather, the average Muslim is more likely to respond with prepackaged Islamic cliches. And frequently, this is done with an air of arrogance that seems to express pity for anyone who dares disagree with his or her pontifications.

On the other hand, I have met genuinely humble Muslims. I would not say they are the norm, but definitely they are found throughout the Islamic world. How refreshing to interact at a deep level with a Muslim who is open to dissenting opinions.

To be fair, a parallel question must be asked: How many Christians are truly humble? Jesus takes cognizance of this universal problem and repeatedly exhorts his followers to brokenness and humility. Regrettably, some of the proudest persons I have ever met have been professing Christians. The quest for true godliness continues.

Eternal Punishment for Dissonance within Community

> Narrated Abu Huraira: The Prophet said, "None of you should point towards his Muslim brother with a weapon, for he does not know, Satan may tempt him to hit him and thus he would fall into a pit of fire (Hell)" (9:153; 88.7.193).

A similar teaching is expressed in this Hadith:

> Narrated Al-Hasan: Allah's Apostle said, "If two Muslims take out their swords to fight each other, then both of them are from the people of the (Hell) Fire" (9:153; 88.10.204).

Any disturbance, nationally or individually, in the *ummah* (community) of Islam is said to be deplorable in the sight of Allah. How can custodians of ultimate and indisputable truth engage in hatred and warfare among themselves? Such behavior's origin is stated to be satanic and the consequence is for the offenders to be assigned to a fiery hell. This punishment is ultimate and eternal, thus depicting how seriously Allah views the sin of dissonance within Islamic society.

A radically different standard seems to apply to an act of violence between a Muslim and a nonbeliever.

> Narrated Abu Juhaifa: Ali said, "No Muslim should be killed in Qisas (equality in punishment) for killing a Kafir (disbeliever)" (9:38; 83.31.50).

As has been illustrated in the last chapter, jihad is Islamically sanctioned. In this Tradition, it is clearly presented that there is no death penalty for a Muslim who kills an unbeliever. In practice, a murderer is often arrested, charged, and within a short time released.

In one country in Asia, a Muslim recently stabbed to death a convert to Christianity. He surrendered to police and loudly proclaimed his justification for such an act: the convert had publicly maligned the Prophet. Immediately, fundamentalist Muslim leaders proclaimed the murderer a hero of Islam and promised to secure his release from jail. There is no evidence whatsoever that the convert had spoken ill of Muhammad. It seems probable that he was killed because of his faith in Christ. My own feeling is that soon this cold-blooded killer will be freely walking the streets of his Muslim nation and will be proclaimed by many to be a true defender of the faith. This sequence of events would flow quite naturally from the Hadith teachings I have presented in these two chapters.

Lapses in Spirituality

Muhammad is depicted as a tough taskmaster in this Tradition:

> Narrated Abu Huraira: Allah's Apostle said, "By Him in Whose Hands my life is, I was about to order the collecting of fire wood and then order someone to pronounce the Adhan for the prayer and then order someone to lead the people in prayer and then I would go from behind and burn the houses of men who did not present themselves for the (compulsory congregational) prayer" (9:250–51; 89.53.330).

Does Islam legislate spirituality? If one prays, is he or she automatically a dedicated follower of Allah? If a man refuses to pray, then can the legitimate penalty be to burn his house? If this Hadith and example of the Prophet were to be followed literally today, I would estimate 95 percent of Muslim men worldwide would be homeless. On the other hand, such a penalty, if enforced, would guarantee a packed attendance at mosques throughout the Muslim world. Apart from Saudi Arabia, there is probably no real police enforcement of the daily prayer ritual. Even in Saudi, it is the "religious police" who take this responsibility upon themselves.

Beating for Drunkenness

> Narrated Abu Huraira: A man who drank wine was brought to the Prophet. The Prophet said, "Beat him!" Abu Huraira added, "So some of us beat him with our hands, and some with their shoes, and some with their garments (by twisting it) like a lash, and then when we finished, someone said to him, 'May Allah disgrace you!'" (8:506; 81.5.768).

Another Hadith refers to the penalty given to the drunken person.

> Narrated As-Saib bin Yazid: During the last period of Umar's caliphate, he used to give the drunk forty lashes; and when drunks become mischievous and disobedient he used to scourge them eighty lashes (8:507; 81.5.770).

Giving lashes as punishment to offending Muslims was clearly prescribed in the Quran and Traditions. As will be seen in the remainder of this chapter, beatings were looked upon as punitive as well as remedial. From time to time photos appear in news magazines of Muslim wrongdoers being whipped by police. The modern world regards this as cruel and excessive. Islamic clerics declare that this response to sin is mandated by Almighty God himself.

Flogging or Stoning for Promiscuity

Sexual promiscuity has always been a target of the wrath of Muslim religious enforcers. But their response is most often confined to the borders of any particular Islamic country. For instance, disco advertisements in Manila are printed in Arabic, especially to accommodate Middle Eastern Muslim tourists. In a large-circulation Manila newspaper, a picture appeared of the daughter of the Saudi ambassador to the Philippines. She was participating as a model in a fashion show that was attended by the male and female elite of the Philippines. She was dressed in a strapless dress. If she appeared in that dress on any street in Saudi, she would immediately be beaten and taken to jail. Why the double standard?

In reality, this hypocrisy is extremely common among men who leave Saudi and are then able to discard the enforced restraints of Islamic morality. To be fair, I do not think Muslim male travelers are any more immoral than are those who would identify themselves as Christians. The problem arises in Islam's profession of moral purity that is backed up by severe penalties for aberrations. But then, such standards are often flagrantly violated in distant and discreet settings.

All of Islam's concern about sexual sin is based on Scripture and Traditions.

Narrated Abu Huraira: The verdict of Allah's Apostle was sought about an unmarried slave girl guilty of illegal sexual intercourse. He replied, "If she commits illegal sexual intercourse, then flog her (one hundred stripes), and if she commits illegal sexual intercourse (after that for the second time), then flog her (a hundred stripes), and if she commits illegal sexual intercourse (for the third time) then flog her (a hundred stripes) and sell her for even a hair rope" (8:548; 82.22.822).

Several Hadith refer to sexual sins. In this Tradition, the unmarried slave girl is flogged one hundred times. This is in agreement with the Quran. No mention is made of a penalty for the male adulterer in this situation.

Narrated Abu Huraira: The Prophet said, "Your son will get a hundred lashes and one year exile." He then addressed somebody, "O Unais! Go to the [adulteress] and stone her to death." So, Unais went and stoned her to death (3:535; 49.5.860).

This Tradition brings up the discrimination between punishments for men and women. The male adulterer will receive physical pain and exile. This is manageable: in one year all he will have to bear is emotional embarrassment. In contrast, the woman is sentenced to death by the painful process of stoning. These words came directly from Muhammad. Why should the man be considered less guilty than the woman? The context, as is usual in the Hadith, gives us no further details. But in many if not most instances in life, the male is the more aggressive person in initiating a sexual encounter. Yet, this man was able to live on, perhaps to once again commit an immoral act. Conversely, the woman suffered an ignominious execution.

In yet another Hadith we see both parties stoned to death. Also we note the basis of authority for this punishment.

Narrated Abdullah bin Umar: The Jews came to Allah's Apostle and told him that a man and a woman from amongst them had committed illegal sexual intercourse. Allah's Apostle said to them, "What do you find in the Torah about the legal punishment of Ar-Rajm (stoning)?" They replied, "We announce their crime and lash them." Abdullah bin Salam said, "You are telling a lie; Torah contains the order of Rajm." They brought and opened the Torah and one of them placed his hand on the Verse of Rajm and read the verses preceding and following it. Abdullah bin Salam said to him, "Lift your hand." When he lifted his hand, the Verse of Rajm was written there. They said, "Muhammad has told the truth; the Torah has the Verse of Rajm." The Prophet then gave the order that both of them should be stoned to death. (Abdullah bin Umar said, "I saw the man leaning over the woman to shelter her from the stones" (4:532–33; 56.25.829).

This incident involves Jews, therefore, the Prophet was keen to have these sinners judged by the law of the Old Testament. This may have led to Muhammad's accepting a non-Quranic punishment for adultery among Muslims, as is found in this rather strange Tradition:

Narrated Jabir: A man from the tribe of Asiam came to the Prophet and confessed that he had committed illegal sexual intercourse. The Prophet turned his face away from him till the man bore witness against himself four times. The Prophet said to him, "Are you mad?" He said, "No." [The Prophet] said, "Are you married?" He said, "Yes." Then the Prophet ordered that he be stoned to death, and he was stoned to death at the Musalla. When the stones troubled him, he fled, but he was caught and was stoned till he died. The Prophet spoke well of him and offered his funeral prayer (8:531; 82.11.810).

For whatever reason, Muhammad did not want to judge this man. The adulterer was evidently smitten in conscience and felt the need of confession and penance. It is interesting to note Muhammad considered this man to be mad for admitting his sin and exposing himself to capital punishment.

This Hadith clearly defines stoning unto death as the penalty for adultery. Modern Islamic jurists who favor stoning refer to Traditions like this to substantiate their opinion. They opt to disregard the Quran on the subject. I am not quite sure how Saudis can give preference to Hadith punishment over the reputed very words of Allah as found in the Quran.

A question could arise as to why Muhammad spoke kindly of the adulterer and then led in his funeral prayer. He had just sentenced the man to a painful death. The only apparent conclusion is that the sinner had confessed and repented of his adultery. He was even prepared for execution. Muhammad's understanding of the law of Allah led him to emphasize punishment over mercy and forgiveness; even though he appreciated the forthright honesty of the sinner.

Amputation of Limbs for Theft

> Narrated Abu Huraira: The Prophet said, "Allah curses a man who steals a Baida (i.e., an egg) and gets his hand cut off, or steals a rope and gets his hand cut off" (8:509; 81.8.774).

The non-Muslim community has always found amputation to be an overly severe punishment for a sin as insignificant as the theft of an egg or a piece of rope. Yet, here we have a clear and definitive word of the Prophet sanctioning and ordering a thief's hand to be cut off. Not only is amputation to be endured, but also the transgressor receives the curse of Allah. In Saudi this practice is legalistically followed. In other Muslim countries, among them Pakistan, there is ongoing debate as to whether amputation is to be meted out to every thief.

It would seem that repentance after the punishment is carried out is acceptable to Muhammad.

> Narrated Urwa Az-Zubair: A woman committed theft in the Ghazwa (attack) of the Conquest (of Mecca) and she was taken to the Prophet who ordered her hand to be cut off. Aisha said, "Her repentance was perfect and she was married (later) and used to come to me (after that) and I would present her needs to Allah's Apostle" (3:496; 48.8.816).

The allusion to the woman's marriage is an insight into the culture of the day. I am surprised that a convicted thief suffering the ongoing embarrassment of amputation could ever find a man to marry her. Many such questions arise as one reads the condensed versions of events as recorded in the Hadith.

Execution and the Principle of Retribution

Retribution as "an eye for an eye and a tooth for a tooth" is illustrated in this incident.

> Narrated Anas: A Jew crushed the head of a girl between two
> stones. The girl was asked who had crushed her head, and some
> names were mentioned before her, and when the name of the Jew
> was mentioned, she nodded agreeing. The Jew was captured and
> when he confessed, the Prophet ordered that his head be crushed
> between two stones (3:352; 41.21.596).

The girl was not killed as a result of her head being crushed. As
the description of the Jew's punishment is the same as what he
had done to the girl, it can be assumed this punishment was not
unto death.

Killing a person with fire is said to be a penalty for wrongdoing that is to be performed only by Allah.

> Narrated Abu Huraira: Allah's Apostle sent us on a military expe-
> dition telling us, "If you find such and such persons (he named two
> men from Quraish), burn them with fire." Then we came to bid
> him farewell, when we wanted to set out, he said, "Previously I
> ordered you to burn so-and-so and so-and-so with fire, but as pun-
> ishment with fire is done by none except Allah, if you capture them,
> kill them, (instead)" (4:127–28; 52.107.202).

Capital punishment was a norm in the time of the Prophet. If
a person lived by the sword, he or she would die by the sword.
But one Hadith is gruesome in its description of an execution of
several men.

> Narrated Anas: So they set out, and when they reached Al-Harra,
> they reverted to Heathenism after embracing Islam, and killed the
> shepherd of the Prophet, and drove away the camels. When this
> news reached the Prophet, he sent some people in pursuit of them.
> (So they were caught and brought back to the Prophet). The
> Prophet gave his orders concerning them. So nails were driven in
> their eyes, and their hands and legs were cut off and they were left
> in Harra until they died in that state of theirs (5:354; 59.35.505).

These men are depicted as engaging in at least three acts: they
turned back to their old religion after having converted to Islam;
they killed a man who evidently worked for Muhammad; they
scattered the Prophet's camels. Knowing the gravity of their
actions, they fled. Soon they were caught and brought to

Muhammad. The Prophet seems to become the judge and jury. We cringe as we read of nails being driven into the men's eyes. Hands and legs are crudely amputated. The punishment was inflicted in the same place where the men were caught. Perhaps this was to serve as a warning to other potential wrongdoers.

Today, in many Western prisons, lethal injections have taken the place of the electric chair, hanging, or the gas chamber. This is in the interest of making capital punishment as humane as possible. Islam still embraces public flogging and amputation of limbs as legitimate punishments. In fact, Muslims are locked into these procedures because of scriptural constraints.

A rather extraordinary event is chronicled in this Hadith.

> Narrated Abu Amir: There will be some people who will stay near the side of a mountain and in the evening their shepherd will come to them with their sheep and ask them for something, but they will say to him, "Return to us tomorrow." Allah will destroy them during the night and will let the mountain fall on them, and He will change the rest of them into monkeys and pigs and they will remain so until the Day of Resurrection (7:345–46; 69.6.494b).

These people are severely judged because they put off a request from their shepherd. As a consequence, some of them are destroyed when a mountain falls on them. Others of the group metamorphose into pigs and monkeys. The evidence that this is not an eschatological happening is that these offenders are to remain as animals until the day of resurrection.

All religions postulate moral codes of conduct with attendant prescribed punishments for aberrations. Islam has done this in tune with the Old Testament, which prescribes that rebellious sons and adulterers are to be stoned to death. The New Testament presents the woman who was caught in the act of adultery being forgiven by Jesus. She is then exhorted to go and sin no more. The world view of Christians has undergone a paradigm shift from the harshness of the Old Testament law to the New Testament emphasis on mercy and forgiveness. How many Christians would support the public stoning to death of an adulterer or a wayward son?

In 1992, the president of Algeria was assassinated because of his opposition to fundamentalist Muslims. The same was true of the murder of President Sadat of Egypt. I fear such unilateral earthly punishments will continue to be meted out to perceived wrongdoers. Islamic Scriptures are a source from which the extremists can selectively pick and choose, thus legitimizing their acts of violence. Such fanatical deeds will continue to be denounced by other Muslim theologians and laypeople who see Islam in a different light.

Once again the Christian message of grace and forgiveness pushes to the fore. Sinners may suffer the dire consequences of sin, but there is a biblical emphasis that assures the transgressor of a new birth if he or she comes humbly in faith to the cross and experiences sins forgiven by Christ's shed blood. Muslims need to be made aware of the contrast between Hadith passages and the account of Jesus as he forgave the woman caught in the act of adultery. I know of one Muslim who picked up a Christian tract from a pool of water by the roadside. He enthusiastically read John 8. This led directly to a salvation experience both for him and for his family. I had the joy of participating in the discipleship of this man who was so impressed with Christ's dealing with an adulterous woman.

Judgment Day

*I*slam has a well-defined and fairly comprehensible theology of future events. There will be a sudden cessation of the world as we know it. Allah will usher in "the Hour," as the moment of judgment is referred to in Islamic Scripture. Muslims will be in the best position on that awesome occasion. Their works will be judged and they will receive punishment. But their faith in Allah and the Prophet ultimately will assure them of eternal life. Those who deny Islam and its beliefs will be sentenced to a gruesome eternity of suffering in the fires of hell.

Muhammad was once given a vision of the future:

> Narrated Anas bin Malik: Once Allah's Apostle led us in prayer and then (after finishing it) ascended the pulpit and pointed with his hand towards the Qibla [direction of prayer] of the mosque and said, "While I was leading you in prayer, both Paradise and Hell were displayed in front of me in the direction of this wall, I had never seen a better thing (than Paradise) and a worse thing (than Hell) as I have seen today" (8:315; 76.18.475).

The more developed eschatological teaching of Islam seems to rely heavily on New Testament rather than Old Testament concepts. As such, judgment, heaven, and hell play a motivating role among Muslims in regard to following religious forms, maintaining personal purity, and carrying out the evangelistic imperative of Islam—at least they should. In practice, however, the realities of future events probably affect the behavior of Muslims about as they do Christians: minimally!

Those of us in the evangelical tradition of Christianity are familiar with the teaching of signs that indicate we are on the threshold of the great apocalyptic event. Bible instructors repeatedly make the case that these indicators are more prevalent now than ever before in the two thousand years since the signs were originally recorded. Islam has its own set of "portents of the Hour" that are to serve as a warning to humankind to prepare for the great final day of judgment.

> Narrated Anas: I heard Allah's Apostle saying: "From among the portents of the Hour are (the following):
>
> 1. Religious knowledge will decrease (by the death of religious learned men).
> 2. Religious ignorance will prevail.
> 3. There will be prevalence of open illegal sexual intercourse.
> 4. Women will increase in number and men will decrease in number so much so that fifty women will be looked after by one man" (1:68; 3.22.81).

The first three signs are rather nebulous and difficult to critique as we overview fourteen hundred years of Islamic history. Number 4, however, creates more than a little bewilderment. A ratio of fifty women to one man seems almost impossible to contemplate. Is war the cause of these disproportionate numbers? In these modern times, even nuclear warfare with its capability of mass destruction would affect both sexes. Muslims agree that there is an element of mystery in this Hadith. But they are quite content to affirm its truth while patiently waiting for its fulfillment.

Muhammad gave a further word regarding the timing of the day of judgment.

> Narrated Sahl: Allah's Apostle said, "I have been sent and the Hour (is at hand) as these two," showing his two fingers and sticking (separating) them out.

[Translator's Note: This means, it will not be long before the Hour takes place. The period between the Prophet and the coming of the Hour will not be long] (8:337; 76.39.510).

The early Christians believed that the New Testament indicated Christ's return was imminent. They looked to the skies for that certain cloud and attuned their ears for that special sound of God's trumpet. Alas, now, nearly two thousand years later, we as believers are still anticipating the "imminent return" of our Savior. We bow before the realization that God's sovereign timetable and even his understanding of time is evidently very different from ours. It also appears it is distinct from that of the many Christian leaders down through the centuries!

Enter Muhammad. He too understood the culmination of the age soon would take place. To my knowledge, Islamic theologians have never set dates for the great apocalyptic event. They are content to live in a state of anticipation.

The Prophet did foresee the Hour occurring with great suddenness.

> Narrated Abu Huraira: Allah's Apostle said, "The Hour will be established (so suddenly) that two persons spreading a garment between them will not be able to finish their bargain, nor will they be able to fold it up. The Hour will be established while a man is carrying the milk of his she-camel, but cannot drink it; and the Hour will be established when someone is not able to prepare the tank to water his livestock from it; and the Hour will be established when some of you has raised his food to his mouth but cannot eat it" (8:339; 76.40.513).

These words closely parallel the words of Christ. It is interesting to note how adherents of both religions agree that the moment of apocalypse will come unannounced and unexpected. Most of humanity will be caught unprepared. This fact doesn't surprise us given the lead-in period of two thousand and fourteen hundred years respectively.

> Narrated Abu Huraira: I heard Allah's Apostle saying, "We (Muslims) are the last (to come) but (will be) the foremost on the Day of Resurrection though the former nations were given the Holy Scriptures before us" (2:1; 13.1.1).

Citations from the Quran and Traditions consistently present Muslims as the favored ones of Allah. The "Holy Scriptures" refers to the Old and New Testaments. Islam was launched six hundred years post-Christ, but Allah abrogated and purified the former Scriptures. Now, Muslims believe, they will stand before Allah as his chosen ones clothed in truth. Even though Jews and Christians are "People of the Book," they have greatly erred by rejecting Muhammad, the Quran, and the Traditions. Such a common belief among Muslims finds direct reinforcement in this Hadith. "The latest and the greatest" is no mere cliché in Islam.

A number of happenings will reportedly unfold during Allah's great hour. Several Hadith set the stage for what will take place.

> Narrated Abu Huraira: The Prophet said, "On the Day of Resurrection Allah will hold the whole earth and fold the heaven with His right hand and say, 'I am the King; where are the kings of the earth?'" (9:355; 93.6.479).

God, according to Muslims, has sovereign rights over his subjects. The kings of the earth will be totally insignificant when the glory of Allah will be fully revealed. No one will be able to withstand his power and authority. Earthly potentates will be forced to bow in subordination to Allah. A new age is ushered in.

> Narrated Abu Huraira: Allah's Apostle said, "The most awful name in Allah's sight on the Day of Resurrection, will be (that of) a man calling himself Malik Al-Amlak (the king of kings)."
>
> [Translator's Note: *Shahan Shah* is a Persian word bearing the same meaning (as Malik Al-Amlak). This indicates that it is forbidden to call oneself by such a name in any language] (8:144; 72.114.224).

The thought is to Allah alone is ascribed the title *king of kings*. No earthly ruler can dare assign to himself power or designations that compete with the almighty and all-sovereign God.

The realities of the last Hour will be overwhelming. In a verse closely parallel to a biblical passage, Muslim believers are assured of delights to come that are beyond normal comprehension.

Narrated Abu Huraira: The Prophet said, "Allah said, 'I have prepared for my pious worshippers such things as no eye has ever
seen, no ear has ever heard of, and nobody has ever thought of.
All that is reserved, besides which, all that you have seen, is nothing'" (6:289; 60.233.303).

Unbelievers, on the other hand, will have much to dread on
that great day.

Narrated Aisha: Allah's Apostle said, "The people will be gathered
barefooted, naked, and uncircumcised." I said, "O Allah's Apostle! Will the men and the women look at each other?" He said,
"The situation will be too hard for them to pay attention to that"
(8:350; 76.45.534).

Normal fleshly appetites will be subdued in the context of fearful
anticipation of judgment and subsequent suffering. The presence
of uncircumcised men indicates that these are all non-Muslims.
Humiliation is a central motif of this sad gathering of people. (As
I read it, I could not help but think back to Auschwitz, where
naked Jews lined up awaiting their turn for a cyanide "bath.")
Islamic theology places every non-Muslim who has lived since
A.D. 632 into this scene. The one exception will be those who have
never been reached with the message of Islam.

Among the major world religions only Islam and Christianity
deal in extreme harshness with those outside their own belief
structures. In the next chapter the Muslim view of hell will be
presented: an abode of terrible suffering that is to be populated
with Christians, Jews, Hindus, Buddhists, Shintoists, and all others who have not become followers of Muhammad.

Another picture of the Hour visualizes people in their despair.

Narrated Abu Huraira: Allah's Apostle said, "The people will sweat
so profusely on the Day of Resurrection that their sweat will sink
seventy cubits deep into the earth, and it will rise up till it reaches
the people's mouths and ears" (8:354; 75.47.539).

Non-Muslims are seen sweating to such an extent that their bodily
fluids filter more than one hundred feet into the soil. Then the
sweat ascends up to the faces of the nonbelievers. All of this, literal

or figurative we do not know, is a glimpse of the extreme fear people will experience as they stand before Allah in judgment.

There is to be a role for an intercessor on the day of resurrection. In one of the longest Traditions recorded by Al-Bukhari, we have Muslims requesting Adam, Noah, Abraham, Moses, and Jesus to mediate for them before Allah. Each of these prophets declares himself unworthy to intercede and points to the next prophet as perhaps being able to assist the believers. Jesus, being the last of these, also speaks of his inadequacy and refers the supplicants to Muhammad. The Prophet then gives this response:

> Narrated Anas: "So they will come to me and I will proceed till I will ask my Lord's permission and I will be given permission. When I see my Lord, I will fall down in prostration and He will let me remain in that state as long as He wishes and then I will be addressed, '(O Muhammad!) Raise your head. Ask, and your request will be granted; say, and your saying will be listened to: intercede, and your intercession will be accepted.' I will raise my head and praise Allah with a saying (i.e. invocation). He will teach me, and then I will intercede. He will fix a limit for me (to intercede for) whom I will admit into Paradise. Then I will come back again to Allah, and when I see my Lord, the same thing will happen to me. And then I will intercede and Allah will fix a limit for me to intercede whom I will let into Paradise, then I will come back for the third time; and then I will come back for the fourth time, and will say, 'None remains in Hell but those whom the Quran has imprisoned (in Hell) and who have been destined to an eternal stay in Hell'" (6:4, 5; 60.3.3).

It is clear from these words that Muhammad has an important ministry to perform. Allah tells the Prophet his words will be heard and his intercession acted upon. But the limits will be fixed by God alone. The result is that hell will receive its due. All who are destined will spend eternity in that abode of suffering. Even Muhammad cannot alter the eternal decrees of damnation as presented in the Quran.

The resurrection of the body presents rational difficulties for Christians and Muslims alike.

Narrated Abu Huraira: The Prophet said, "Everything of the human body will decay except the coccyx bone (of the tail) and from that bone Allah will reconstruct the whole body" (6:319; 60.254.338).

Islam, through the Prophet, declares that the decayed body will be reconstructed from one bone. Medically speaking, this Hadith is not correct. All major bones deteriorate at the same rate. But the main point is that it is Allah who will bring about a renewed body. It should be noted that Muslims always bury their dead. They do not allow cremation.

It is right to interact with Muslims on this crucial subject. The stakes are high. Eternal life and eternal damnation are core teachings within both Christianity and Islam. There will be a willingness on the part of Muslims to explain their view of the great judgment day. Likewise, they will most probably listen attentively to your presentation.

From this rather melancholic theme, we proceed downward and enter into a discussion on the terrors of hell.

ell

*T*he reality of hell, for many, is speculative. No one has ever visited the everlasting fires and returned to earth to give a dramatic first-hand report of his or her findings. But for Christians and Muslims the existence of hell is confirmed by Scripture. Old Testament passages are somewhat vague on the subject, whereas the New Testament clearly presents hell as a place of ongoing suffering. Quranic and Hadith citations are even more pungently descriptive concerning the abode of the nonbelievers and the unrighteous.

My observations lead me to conclude that Christians interact academically with the concept of hell more than do Muslims. New Testament theologians have been known to water down the fires of hell by declaring the place to be symbolic rather than literal. Others attach purgatory to the teaching in order to shorten the duration of suffering. Still others have changed the words *eternal* and *everlasting* into a doctrine that sets forth hell as a place of annihilation.

No such problem exists for Muslims. Perhaps the historical roots of Islam along with the teaching of jihad make it easier for Muslims to concur with the repetitive teaching on hell as found in their Scriptures. I have never met a Muslim who has attempted to undercut the bluntness and severity of their doctrine of hell.

For most, it appears there is a smug satisfaction that sinners will at last receive their deserved punishment.

Theology and Descriptions of Hell

The Hadith compares the fires of hell to ordinary fire as found in everyday life.

> Narrated Abu Huraira: Allah's Apostle said, "Your (ordinary) fire is one of 70 parts of the (Hell) Fire." Someone asked, "O Allah's Apostle! This (ordinary) fire would have been sufficient (to torture the unbelievers)." Allah's Apostle said, "The (Hell) Fire has 69 parts more than the ordinary (worldly) fire, each part is as hot as this (worldly) fire" (4:315; 54.9.487).

The disciples of Muhammad could hardly imagine a fire with "69 parts" more than the fire common to their usage. They wondered aloud if so much heat was necessary.

> Narrated Abu Huraira: Allah's Apostle said, "The (Hell) Fire complained to its Lord saying, 'O my Lord! My different parts eat up each other.' So, He allowed it to take two breaths, one in the winter and the other in summer, and this is the cause of the severe heat and the bitter cold you find (in weather)" (4:313–14; 54.9.482).

In this Tradition fire takes on an anthropomorphic dimension and registers a complaint to God. It seems hell is segmented and because of its intense heat is self-destructing. The response given by Allah is to allow a release of the build-up of heat. What is difficult to comprehend is how these "two breaths" can produce opposite results, one being summer and extreme heat, and the other winter and bitter cold.

> Narrated Abu Dhar: While the Prophet was on a journey, he said (regarding the performance of the Zuhr prayer), "Wait till it (i.e. the weather) gets cooler." He said the same again till the shade of the hillocks extended. Then he said, "Delay the Zuhr Prayer till it gets cooler, for the severity of heat is due to the increase in the flames of Hell and comes out of its heat" (4:313; 54.9.480).

Here the Prophet attributes Arabia's hot weather to the increase in the flames of hell. Muhammad's theology and pronouncements would probably have undergone major revision if he could have traveled more widely. His ethnocentrism would have been muted by a trip to Alaska or the Antarctic. It was easy, living in the 110°F temperature of the blazing desert, to comprehend the fires of hell and subsequently to blame present discomfort on an overspill from the netherworld.

Muhammad often denounces riches as being an instrument of Satan to seduce believers from the straight path of Allah.

Narrated Ibn Abi Laila: The Prophet forbade us to wear clothes of silk or Dibaj, and to drink out of gold or silver vessels, and said, "These things are for them (unbelievers) in this world and for you (Muslims) in the Hereafter. . . . He who drinks from a silver vessel is but filling his abdomen with Hell Fire" (7:366–67; 69.28.538).

The fire of hell is depicted as indwelling the profligate person. Conversely, the true believer is to dress modestly and use basic household items. But in the future nothing will be withheld from faithful Muslims. Silver and gold vessels are but small tokens of the riches to be received in the life to come.

Narrated Sahl: The Prophet said, "Fire, and verily (the rewards of) the deeds are decided by the last actions (deeds)" (8:395; 77.4.604).

How one ends life's journey is extremely important for the Muslim. His or her last deeds will be eternally determinative. This does not mean early actions will be disregarded. But assessment depends on how one finishes. How sobering this thought is as we ponder the many religious people who have struggled to maintain a life of purity but in their waning years have strayed far from the narrow path of moral integrity.

Narrated Ibn Abbas: Once the Prophet, while passing through one of the grave-yards of Medina or Mecca heard the voices of two persons who were being tortured in their graves. The Prophet said, "These two persons are being tortured not for a major sin (to avoid)." The Prophet then added, "Yes! (they are being tortured for a major sin). Indeed, one of them never saved himself from being soiled with his urine while the other used to go about with calumnies (to make enmity between friends)." The Prophet then asked for a green leaf of a date-palm tree, broke it into two pieces and put one on each grave. On being asked why he had done so, he replied, "I hope that their torture might be lessened, till these get dried" (1:141; 4.57.215).

The Hadith frequently alludes to sounds rising from dead Muslims and being heard by people walking through a cemetery. Most common is for these cries to originate from the deceased who are being tortured in hell. In this Tradition, one of the persons is being punished because of his failure to follow the Islamic ritual of water cleansing following urination. How trivial a "sin" to bring about such a severe judgment. Muhammad at first declared this omission as a minor transgression, then changed his mind and stated it was indeed a major sin. One would like to receive a fuller explanation as to how neglecting a washing ritual can destine a person to physical torment in the afterlife. But this again highlights the extreme importance of legalistic minutiae within Islam.

The Prophet then performed a simple act that seems puzzling to the outsider. What effect, scientifically, could one expect to result from placing the green leaf of a date palm tree on the graves of two Muslims who are undergoing torture? Even the relief was to be temporary. It was only to last only until the leaf became dry. Muhammad himself seemed unsure of the eventual outcome of his act. The Prophet's "hope" was that the suffering ones would receive a measure of comfort.

A rather startling Tradition has Abraham's father turned into an animal and thrown into the fires of hell.

Narrated Abu Huraira: The Prophet said, "On the Day of Resurrection Abraham will meet his father Azar whose face will be dark and covered with dust. (The Prophet) Abraham will say (to him): 'Didn't I tell you not to disobey me?' His father will reply: 'Today I will not disobey you.' Abraham will say: 'O Lord! You promised not to disgrace me on the Day of Resurrection; and what will be more disgraceful to me than cursing and dishonoring my father?' Then Allah will say (to him): 'I had forbidden Paradise to the infidels.' Then he will be addressed, 'O Abraham! Look! What is underneath your feet?' He will look and there he will see a Dhabh (an animal) blood-stained, which will be caught by the legs and thrown in the (Hell) Fire."

[Translator's Note: Abraham's father will be transformed into an animal and thrown into the Fire; for his Muslim son's intercession will not avail, as he was an infidel. Abraham then will repudiate his father] (4:365; 55.9.569).

The high price of being an infidel is poignantly described in these few words. Abraham's father refused the witness of his son during his lifetime. On the great day of resurrection there is to be no second chance. The father is now ready to obey Abraham, but it is too late. Destiny has been sealed. The note following the Hadith offers further explanation. Abraham is an extremely popular prophet for Muslims. To think of him interacting with his father in this manner is both strange and shocking. Especially is this true in light of Islamic teaching concerning the respect that is to be given to one's parents.

Narrated Usama: The Prophet said, "I stood at the gate of the Fire and found that the majority of the people entering it were women" (8:363; 76.51.555).

Evidently in this Tradition, Muhammad is having a prophetical vision relating to the day of judgment. In actual fact, more women in Islam are religiously devout and meticulous in following rituals than are Muslim men. I have often admired their hard work and patience as they have had to endure very demanding husbands. Empirically speaking, I would be prone to turn the Hadith around and see the majority of Muslim women entering Paradise.

Narrated Ibu Umar: The Prophet said, "A woman entered the (Hell) Fire because of a cat which she had tied, neither giving it food nor setting it free to eat from the vermin of the earth" (4:337; 54.15.535).

What a severe penalty this woman is paying because of her neglect of a cat. It is difficult to ponder why the everlasting fires of hell should be prescribed for such an offense. Does this Hadith not relegate a woman to a low status? It would appear she is not as important as a cat.

A widely held belief in Islam centers around a bridge that spans the raging torrents of hellfire below.

> Narrated Abu Huraira: The Prophet said, "Then a bridge will be laid over the (Hell) Fire." Allah's Apostle added, "I will be the first to cross it. And the invocation of the Apostles on that Day, will be: Allahumma Sallim, Sallim (O Allah, save us, save us!), and over that bridge there will be hooks similar to the thorns of As-Sadan (a thorny tree). Didn't you see the thorns of As-Sadan?" The companions said, "Yes, O Allah's Apostle." He added, "So the hooks over that bridge will be like the thorns of As-Sadan except that their greatness in size is only known to Allah. The hooks will snatch the people according to their deeds: Some people will be ruined because of their evil deeds, and some will be cut into pieces and fall down in Hell, but will be saved afterwards, when Allah has finished the judgments among His slaves, and intends to take out of the Fire whoever He wishes to take out from among those who used to testify that none had the right to be worshipped but Allah. He will order the angels to take them out and the angels will know them by the mark of the traces of prostration (on their foreheads) for Allah banned the Fire to consume the traces of prostration on the body of Adam's son. So they will take them out, and by then they would have been burned (as coal), and then water, called Maul Hayat (water of life) will be poured on them, and they will spring out like a seed springs out on the bank of a rainwater stream" (8:375–76; 76.52.577).

This is a descriptive insight into the happenings of the great day of judgment. Muhammad will lead the way across the bridge. His will be the honored position, above that of all other prophets. This is in keeping with the dogmatic assertion that Muhammad is the greatest of all the true spokesmen of Allah.

Some Muslims will be cut up and thrown into hell. But fortunate for them, their sojourn there is comparable to that of a backslidden Roman Catholic in purgatory. After a measure of suffering and purging, the Muslim will be released. One of the determinants as to duration of punishment relates to how faithful the Muslim has been in his or her prayer life. I have observed Iranian Muslims prostrate in prayer in such a manner that their forehead touches a small stone that has been placed in just the correct position on the prayer rug. By connecting in this way, over a period of time a visible indentation appears on the forehead. Allah is said to have made this mark permanent. It becomes their passport into paradise.

The renewed and restored believers are then refreshed with the water of life being poured over them. They are now ready to enter into all the delights that have been prepared for those who have a prevailing love for Allah. Redemption is at last complete. It is commonly believed by Muslims that even the worst sinner among them will eventually be released from hell. A further Hadith alludes to the subject:

> Narrated Abu Said Al-Khudri: The Prophet said, "When the people of Paradise will enter Paradise and the people of Hell will go to Hell, Allah will order those who have had faith equal to the weight of a grain of mustard seed to be taken out from Hell. So they will be taken out but (by then) they will have been blackened (charred) so they will be put in the river of Haya (rain)" (1:24; 2.15.21).

Faith being compared to a grain of mustard seed appears to be biblical in origin. In this Hadith such a small amount of faith provides an escape from hell. The charred Muslim will then be cleansed with water.

Suicide is strictly prohibited within Islam. Two Hadith are presented as representational of the penalty prescribed for the person who willfully takes his life.

> Narrated Abu Huraira: The Prophet said, "Whoever purposely throws himself from a mountain and kills himself will be in the (Hell) Fire falling down into it and abiding therein perpetually forever; and whoever drinks poison and kills himself with it, he will be carrying his poison in his hand and drinking it in the (Hell) Fire wherein he will abide eternally forever; and whoever kills himself with an iron weapon, will be carrying that weapon in his hand and stabbing his abdomen with it in the (Hell) Fire wherein he will abide eternally forever" (7:450–51; 71.56.670).

> Narrated Jundub: Allah's Apostle said, "Amongst the nations before you there was a man who got a wound, and growing impatient (with its pain), he took a knife and cut his hand with it and the blood did not stop till he died. Allah said, 'My Slave hurried to

bring death upon himself so I have forbidden him (to enter) Paradise'" (4:442–43; 55.45.669).

The penalty for a Muslim's taking his life is severe indeed. Perpetual hellfire will be the abode of the one who dares violate God's decree against self-destruction. Guilty parties will drink poison and continue stabbing themselves throughout eternity. This view somewhat parallels the practice of the Roman Catholic Church, which denies a Christian funeral for the person who has taken his or her life.

Behind this dogmatic position lies a theological premise. Allah alone can give life and only he is allowed to take it. God may use illness, accidents, or even violence to terminate life. That is his prerogative. But death is never to be self-induced. If it is, there will be an eternal price to pay for such willful disobedience.

Statistics relating to the frequency of Muslim suicide are difficult to obtain. Families seek to attribute death to other causes. Governments are inept when it comes to compiling such statistics. Causes of suicide relate to economic issues as well as to relational conflicts. Often I have read of a jilted lover taking her life as she could not bear the hurt of rejection. In rural areas of one Muslim country the instrument of choice is usually rat poison, although self-arranged hangings are fairly common. It is my considered opinion, however, that suicides are more frequent in Western countries than in Islamic nations.

Tortures in Hell

Abu Talib was Muhammad's uncle, guardian, and friend. It was a grief to the Prophet that one so close to him never converted to Islam. This concern is reflected in a Hadith that mentions Abu Talib.

> Narrated Abu Said Al-Khudri that he heard the Prophet mentioning his uncle (i.e. Abu Talib). "Perhaps my intercession will be helpful to him on the Day of Resurrection so that he may be put in a shallow fire reaching only up to his ankles making his brain boil" (5:141–42; 58.39.224).

Muhammad once again indicates awareness of his intercessory power. He will seek to utilize it in behalf of his beloved uncle. But even Muhammad's prayer has limitations. The fire that reaches to Abu Talib's ankles will have the force to make his brain boil. On occasions like this one would expect more of an emotional reaction from Muhammad. How terrible it would be to ponder such a fate of a dearly loved relative. But true to the norm, Muhammad expresses no emotion or regret. This is simply accepted as the will of Allah.

> Narrated An-Numan: I heard the Prophet saying, "The least pun-ished person of the Hell Fire people on the Day of Resurrection, will be a man under whose arch of the feet a smouldering ember will be placed so that his brain will boil because of it" (8:368; 76.51.566).

Boiling brains are mentioned in a number of Hadith. It is as though the slightest heat to be applied at the lower part of the body will work up to the brain and cause it to boil. If this torture is prescribed for "the least punished person," one can only imagine what is meted out as greater punishment.

> Narrated Ibn Abbas: The Prophet said, "Whoever claims to have seen a dream which he did not see, will be ordered to make a knot between two barley grains which he will not be able to do; and if somebody listens to the talk of some people who do not like him (to listen) or they run away from him, then molten lead will be poured into his ears on the Day of Resurrection; and whoever makes a picture, will be punished on the Day of Resurrection and will be ordered to put a soul in that picture, which he will not be able to do" (9:134; 87.45.165).

Two of these retributive acts seem to lead more to frustration than suffering. Sinners will be ordered to do that which they cannot accomplish. The more severe punishment is reserved for a person who overhears secret words. On the day of resurrection this sinner is to have molten lead poured into his ears. One can imagine this also leads to boiled brains!

> Narrated Abu Wail: The Prophet said: "A man will be brought on the Day of Resurrection and thrown in the (Hell) fire, so that his

intestines will come out, and he will go around like a donkey goes around a millstone. The people of (Hell) Fire will gather around him and say: 'O so-and-so! What is wrong with you? Didn't you order us to do good deeds and forbid us to do bad deeds?' He will reply: 'Yes, I used to order you to do good deeds, but I did not do them myself, and I used to forbid you to do bad deeds, yet I used to do them myself'" (4:316; 54.9.489).

Hypocrisy carries with it an extreme penalty. With intestines protruding outward, the sinner is made to go around hell confessing to people that he held to a double standard in life. His demands of others did not match his own deeds.

There is another story of a man in hell with an intestinal problem:

Narrated Abu Huraira: The Prophet said, "I saw Amr bin Amir bin Luhai Al-Khuza'i dragging his intestines in the (Hell) fire, for he was the first man who started the custom of releasing animals (for the sake of false gods)" (4:473; 56.9.723).

It is not completely clear what it means to "release animals." Perhaps the reference is to the sacrifice of animals to false gods. Or it could refer to being a supplier of animals for this purpose. In any event, it is a serious sin that leads to a painful experience in hell.

Narrated Anas: The Prophet said, "Then he will be hit with an iron hammer between his two ears, and he will cry and that cry will be heard by whatever approaches him except human beings and jinns" (2:236; 23.66.422).

An iron hammer is another instrument used to inflict pain and punishment. The description is explicit even to the type of hammer and where the person will be hit. It is unclear why humans and jinns (spiritual beings) will not hear the cry of the sinner. I'm not sure who or what will be in hell besides humans and jinns. Another esoteric reference:

Narrated Abu Said Al-Khudri: The Prophet said, "At that time every pregnant female shall drop her load (have a miscarriage) and a child will have grey hair. And you shall see mankind as in a drunken state, yet not drunk, but severe will be the torment of Allah" (6:238; 60.205.265).

This reference is alluding to the coming great and awful day of judgment. It will be a terrible time of destruction, desolation, and deprivation. So severe will be the fear that the hair of apprehensive children will turn gray. Mankind will reel about as drunks.

A colorful Hadith adds to the chronicle of pain that will be endured by the unrighteous.

> Narrated Abu Huraira: Allah's Apostle said, "On the Day of Resurrection the Kanz (Treasure or wealth of which Zakat has not been paid) of anyone of you will appear in the shape of a huge bald headed poisonous male snake and its owner will run away from it, but it will follow him and say, 'I am your Kanz.'" The Prophet added, "By Allah, that snake will keep on following him until he stretches out his hand and lets the snake swallow it" (9:73–74; 86.3.89).

Here we have described the penalty for personal greed. The selfish person will flee from an incarnation of the Kanz, which becomes a poisonous snake. Harassment continues until finally the snake is pacified by swallowing the man's hand.

From this rather dreary subject we move on to the more enticing and exciting prospects of a future in the sensual delights of paradise that are said to be especially reserved for the true believers in Islam.

13

*P*aradise

*M*uslims are prone to identify emotionally and theologically with heaven rather than hell. Paradise is their long-anticipated abode. At last they will receive their reward for adherence to the "straight path" of Islam. Paradise is depicted in the Quran and Hadith as a totally sinless place of beauty and physical fulfillment with no more struggle, hurt, pain, or sorrow. All will be light and joy. Above all else will be the delight of basking in the eternal presence of Allah. Satan is banished forever. Only righteousness and peace will prevail.

Many picturesque and graphic Hadith outside of Al-Bukhari focus on the sensual and the sexual delights in paradise. I have omitted any of these titillating references, even though they are commonly referred to among Muslim men. In the interest of conservative scholarship, I limit my comments to that which is found in the authoritative collection of Al-Bukhari.

Theology and Description of Heaven

Heaven is reputed to be the exclusive domain of Muslims. Various Quranic and Hadith citations speak approvingly of the "People of the Book" (Jews and Christians), but they are never permitted a place in paradise. Muslims believe they themselves will finally experience the ultimate ummah (community) experience. Purity of belief will make heaven a place free of religious conflict.

> Narrated Abu Huraira: Then he [Muhammad] ordered Bilal to announce amongst the people: "None will enter Paradise but a Muslim soul, and Allah may support this religion (i.e. Islam) even with an evil wicked man" (4:190; 52.182.297).

Allah is said to support Islam with evil men. This Tradition contains ambiguity. Does this backing refer to hypocritical proclamation or financial gifts . . . or both? I recall an outstanding Christian leader who refused a significant monetary gift for his church building project from a liquor wholesaler. The Christian felt his stand against alcohol would be compromised if he accepted such a donation. Evidently Islam gives approval to assistance from nonbelievers. This, of course, does not mean the evil person would earn the privilege to go to paradise.

> Narrated Imran bin Husain: The Prophet said, "I looked at Paradise and found poor people forming the majority of its inhabitants" (4:305; 54.2.464).

In the former chapter we saw the majority of the inhabitants of hell were women. By process of elimination, one could surmise men are to be the majority in heaven. This is not stated. However, most references to paradise seem slanted toward the male sex. This Hadith informs us that the poor will form the largest bloc of people in heaven. One understanding of this Tradition is that the majority of Muslims in the world are poor, at least by comparison to Westerners. It then follows that this will be the most populous group in Paradise.

> Narrated Abu Huraira: The Prophet said, "Paradise and the Fire argued, and the Fire said, 'I have been given the privilege of receiving the arrogant and the tyrants.' Paradise said, 'What is the matter with me? Why do only the weak and the humble among the people enter me?' On that, Allah said to Paradise, 'You are My Mercy which I bestow on whoever I wish of my servants'" (6:354; 60.278.373).

In this Hadith paradise anthropomorphically complains that it is the recipient of only the weak and humble. The people inhabiting heaven are in stark contrast to those in hell, who are said to be arrogant. From this discourse it can be deduced that Muslims give higher spiritual value to humility.

> Narrated Abu Huraira: The Prophet said, "None will enter Paradise but will be shown the place he would have occupied in the (Hell) Fire if he had rejected faith, so that he may be more thankful; and none will enter the (Hell) Fire but will be shown the place he would have occupied in Paradise if he had faith, so that may be a cause of sorrow for him" (8:372–73; 76.51.573).

Sorrow upon entering into hell is compounded by a glimpse into heaven. Conversely, thankfulness is experienced as the believer is allowed to survey the terrors of hell as he enters into the delights of heaven. This Hadith seems to highlight the great gulf between the two eternal abodes. There is a high level of consciousness and understanding on the part of the resurrected. The picture drawn is one of antithesis between two eternal choices.

> Narrated Abu Said Al-Khudri: Allah's Apostle said, "When the believers pass safely over (the bridge across) Hell, they will be stopped at a bridge in between Hell and Paradise where they will retaliate upon each other for the injustices done among them in the world, and when they get purified of all their sins, they will be admitted into Paradise" (3:371; 43.2.620).

Once again we are confronted with a rather ambiguous Tradition. What does it mean that Muslim believers will "retaliate upon each other"? Are the "injustices" a reference to disagreements between believers while they were alive? When this retaliation process is completed it would appear the Muslims will be purged of sins and made ready for heaven. Purgatory seems to be a place as well as a process through which Muslims are cleansed and prepared for an eternity in paradise.

The soldier who fights for Allah and the martyr will have a prominent place in heaven.

> Narrated Abu Huraira: The Prophet said, "Paradise has one-hundred grades which Allah has reserved for the Mujahidun (men who

fight in His Cause), and the distance between each of two grades is like the distance between the Heaven and the Earth" (4:40; 52.4.48).

Narrated Anas Bin Malik: The Prophet said, "Nobody who dies and finds good from Allah (in the Here-after) would wish to come back to this world even if he were given the whole world and whatever is in it, except the martyr who, on seeing the superiority of martyrdom, would like to come back to the world and get killed again (in Allah's cause)" (4:42; 52.6.53).

In the context of Muhammad's historical period, martyrdom meant following the leadership of the Prophet, killing his enemies, and spreading the message of Islam. In this process if one died, he would immediately be ushered into heaven and enjoy a priority status there within the one hundred grades, the meaning of which is unclear. So exhilarating is this process that the martyr would be delighted to relive his life and death.

Rewards in Heaven

Islam teaches that living a righteous life is not an easy task. Five times of daily prayer and one month of fasting are exercises of intense discipline. Satan is always seeking to destroy the believer. Into the midst of this battle Islam introduces a vibrant hope for the future. There will be a most fulfilling eternal reward for the faithful.

Narrated Abu Huraira: Allah's Apostle said, "The first batch (of people) who will enter Paradise will be (glittering) like a full moon; and those who will enter next will be (glittering) like the brightest star. Their hearts will be as if the heart of a single man, for they will have no enmity amongst themselves, and everyone of them shall have two wives, each of whom will be so beautiful, pure, and transparent that the marrow of the bones of their legs will be seen through the flesh. They will be glorifying Allah in the morning and evening, and will never fall ill, and they will neither blow their noses, nor spit. Their utensils will be of gold and silver, and their combs will be of gold, and the matter used in their censers will be the aloes-wood, and their sweat will smell like musk" (4:307–8; 54.7.469).

A number of interesting points are made in this Hadith. Picturesque language about nature depicts joy and happiness. There will be an absence of enmity and conflict among the inhabitants of Paradise. In heaven, unclean bodily functions, along with illness, will be nonexistent. Body odor will be that of musk. Gold and silver will abound. One of the main functions in paradise will be spending time in glorifying Allah.

A feminist may protest this passage. It is written as though only men will be in heaven to enjoy these special privileges. Each man will possess two wives. Other non-Bukhari Hadith refer to seventy-two wives for each husband. These are the houris who are reputed to be special creations of God for the eternal enjoyment of Muslim men. These women remain young and beautiful. But there is no reference anywhere in Islamic writings to suggest Muslim women in heaven will have husbands or even a husband. In fact, there are few specific references to women being in paradise. Rather, they are said to be included in "people" who are in heaven. One can assume they will not recognize their earthly husband in his role as spouse to two new wives.

A similar Hadith adds a few details.

> Narrated Abu Huraira: Allah's Apostle said, "The first group of people who will enter Paradise, will be glittering like the full moon, and those who will follow them, will glitter like the most brilliant star in the sky. They will not urinate, relieve nature, spit, or have any nasal secretions. Their combs will be of gold, and their sweat will smell like musk. The aloes-wood will be used in their censers. Their wives will be houris. All of them will look alike and will resemble their father Adam (in stature), sixty cubits tall" (4:343; 55.1.544).

It appears the last sentence refers to men, who will be ninety feet tall and all will bear semblance to Adam. So there is a distinct uniformity in paradise. One can only speculate as to the height of the houris and other women.

Both in the Quran and the Hadith there are references to heavenly weddings. There is no amplification as to the nature of the ceremony. One scholar of Islam has postulated that Muslim men in this life could become jealous if they thought their wife (or wives) would be married to other men throughout eternity. Thus, the deletion of this subject in Islamic Scriptures. But, conversely, why should Muslim women not feel discriminated against as they ponder their husband's new life in paradise?

> Narrated Anas: The Prophet said, "If a houri from Paradise appeared to the people of the earth, she would fill the space between Heaven and the Earth with light and pleasant scent and her head cover is better than the world and whatever is in it" (4:42; 52.6.53).

Why should happily married men be encouraged to contemplate a timeless eternity of cavorting with new wives who are presented as sensual, charming, and eternally youthful? Does this not undercut the sanctity of one's present marriage?

> Narrated Qais: Allah's Apostle said, "In Paradise there is a pavilion made of a single hollow pearl sixty miles wide, in each corner of which there are wives who will not see those in the other corners; and the believers will visit and enjoy them. And there are two gardens, the utensils and contents of which are made of silver; and two other gardens, the utensils and contents of which are made of so-and-so (i.e. gold) and nothing will prevent the people staying in the Garden of Eden from seeing their Lord except the curtain of majesty over His Face" (6:374; 60.294.402).

Paradise is here referred to as the garden of Eden. In this garden is a pavilion of pleasure where it seems wives are kept in separate corners where they can be discreetly visited by their husbands. The usual utensils of gold and silver are mentioned.

In Islam, Allah is regarded as a spirit. Yet, here in explicit anthropomorphic terms, God is referred to as having a curtain of majesty over his face. This veil is the only obstacle a Muslim encounters in his desire to see Allah. The reader is left to ponder how this seeming contradiction of spirit and flesh comes together. Christians face a similar dilemma in the biblical presentation of God.

> Narrated Abu Huraira: The Prophet said, "In Paradise there is a tree which is so big that a rider can travel in its shade for one hundred years without passing it" (6:376; 60.295.403).

Such a massive tree is hardly imaginable. Certainly shade was a desirable commodity in the desert. To have such a huge area of covering as protection would be considered a great asset throughout eternity.

> Narrated Abdullah bin Amr: The Prophet said, "My Lake-Fount is (so large that it takes) a month's journey to cross it. Its water is whiter than milk, and its smell is nicer than musk (a kind of perfume), and its drinking cups are (as numerous) as the stars of the sky; and whoever drinks from it, will never be thirsty" (8:380; 76.53.581).

Again the Arab value of a scarce item such as water is highlighted. This great body of water is described in terms of color, smell, and function. Even drinking cups will be provided. The promise that the faithful "will never be thirsty" is similar to a biblical passage that assures believers who drink of the water of life that they will never thirst again.

> Narrated Al-Bara: When Ibrahim (the son of the Prophet) died, Allah's Apostle said, "There is a wet nurse for him in Paradise" (8:139; 73.109.215).

Muhammad's sons all died at young ages. His concern for Ibrahim was mediated by the fact that a nurse would be available who would breast-feed him in heaven.

How literally do Muslims believe these rather specific descriptions of paradise? The answer varies. Some emphasize faith and absolutely refuse to think of Quranic and Hadith passages in terms of allegorical or symbolic literary genre. Others are mildly embarrassed with certain Islamic Scriptures and hasten to assign them to a contextual interpretation or to a figurative hermeneutic.

The Muslim view of heaven conceptually parallels the Christian understanding. There will be eternal rewards for the faithful believer. In light of this common belief, it is a natural opening for dialogue between the Christian and the Muslim. The focus can move from the specifics of what is to be found in heaven to the more important issue of how one gains assurance of entry into such a blessed abode. Biblical passages can highlight the Christian position.

14

The Supernatural World

*R*eligion is generally defined as "an interaction between humans and the supernatural." Devotion may be directed toward one of millions of gods by the Hindu, or toward Jesus by the devout Christian, or toward Allah by the Muslim. The supernatural takes us beyond the norm of life. Faith becomes the catalyst that energizes a relationship between the created and the One (or ones) who is deemed to be creator and sustainer of life.

Christianity and Islam both have within their structures a kind of release mechanism for adherents who are mystical in orientation. Islam has scores of millions of Sufi believers within its worldwide community. These disciples can be found expressing their love for God in heartfelt emotional outpourings of worship. Their longing is for a dynamic encounter and experience with their Beloved. Sufis are tolerated amazingly well by mainstream, formalistic Islam.

Pentecostals and charismatics are the Christian counterpart to Sufis. Their more emotional church services with an emphasis on the spirit world of angels and demons have generally been accepted, if not authenticated, by more traditional Christian denominations.

Both Muslim and Christian mystics base their faith and actions on their own particular hermeneutic of Scripture. Sufis are confident the Quran and Hadith make a strong case for an intimate and intensely personal relationship with Allah. Charismatics emphasize certain biblical passages as well as a small collection of writings of early church fathers.

The Hadith presents mystical material that is unknown to the average Muslim. Much of what follows in this chapter will seem both magical and superstitious. Questions will be raised as to whether some of the practices described are not a form of animism. The reader can ponder these Traditions and then make his or her own judgment.

> Narrated Aisha: Some people asked the Prophet regarding the soothsayers. He said, "They are nothing." They said, "O Allah's Apostle! Some of their talks come true." The Prophet said, "That word which happens to be true is what a Jinn snatches away by stealth (from Heaven) and pours it in the ears of his friend (the foreteller) with a sound like the cackling of a hen. The soothsayers then mix with that word, one hundred lies" (9:488; 93.58.650).

This is an interesting explanation of why soothsayers are able to predict future events. A jinn is seen as a coconspirator as he steals truth from heaven. The foreteller is depicted as a friend of the jinn, a not so unnatural alliance as both are intimate with the supernatural. This truth of heavenly insight is then perverted by mixing it with falsehoods. The result is that the soothsayer foretells of that which is true along with that which is false. A skeptic could observe that the soothsayer is simply a good guesser!

> Narrated Um Salama that the Prophet saw in her house a girl whose face had a black spot. He said, "She is under the effect of an evil eye, so treat her with Ruqya (exorcism)" (7:426; 71.35.635).

Muhammad is presented as a person of spiritual discernment in this Hadith. A somewhat disfigured face is stated to be the result of a curse upon the girl. Prescribed treatment was to be the casting out of the evil force in the girl's life. Does this imply that every woman who has a black spot on her face is to be considered a person under a curse? Or is the point being made that the

Prophet, in his unique understanding of spiritual powers, is able to identify that which is demonic contrasted to that which is a natural phenomenon?

> Narrated Sad: Allah's Apostle said, "He who eats seven Ajwa dates every morning, will not be affected by poison or magic on the day he eats them" (7:260; 65.44.356).

Such a safeguard against evil seems more superstition than science. But is it much different than a series of amulets I was offered in a remote Muslim village? The salesman dogmatically assured me that verses of the Quran stuffed in a metal case and worn around my arm or neck would guarantee my immunity to all forms of debilitating disease.

As Christians have we not used and abused the wearing of the ornamental cross as a protective device? And how many young men in battle place a New Testament in their shirt pocket as a symbolic plea for the God of all power to bring them safely through the ravages of war? Perhaps this Hadith strikes us so forcefully because eating dates seems such a mundane, even frivolous way to gain protection from magic and poison.

> Narrated Abu Huraira: The Prophet said, "There are angels at the mountain passes of Medina (so that) neither plague nor Ad-Dajja (religious imposters) can enter it" (9:186; 88.28.247).

The city of Medina played an important role in the life of the Prophet. His sojourn in this city is celebrated in Muslim folklore. Muhammad's military exploits while based in Medina are enthusiastically recounted by the faithful. To Muslims, it is obvious Allah was protecting and blessing the Prophet in the holy city where he would later be buried.

Muhammad, in this Hadith, is able to attribute his protection to the heavenly presence of angels. There is no indication that these heavenly beings were seen by anyone. Most organized religions have a similar teaching concerning the role of protective spirits.

Another Hadith presents a rather strange occurrence.

Narrated Abu Huraira: The Prophet said, "When Allah has
ordained some affair in Heaven, the angels beat (flapped) with
their wings in obedience to His statement, which sounds like a
chain dragged over a rock" (6:187; 60.169.223).

It would appear the angels respond obsequiously to the Word
of Allah. We even have a description of the sound of the flapping
of their wings. But in fact all of this is quite mild in comparison
to the visions recorded in the first few chapters of Ezekiel. The
supernatural emphasis of religions causes believers to see and
experience that which is often both unique and spectacular.

Satan

In Islam, the antithetical force to all that is good and commendable in life is epitomized in the concept of Satan. But how
do Muslims deal with Satan and his influence on a grassroots
level? The Hadith that follow give a small window of insight into
the practical outworkings of this relationship between man and
his hated adversary.

Narrated Ali bin Al-Husain: The Prophet said, "Satan reaches
everywhere in the human body as blood reaches everywhere in
one's body" (3:140; 33.8.251).

Is the Prophet talking about an actual indwelling or is he referring to a type of pervasive influence? Is this true for Muslims
and for non-Muslims? While much is not clear on this subject,
what is commonly accepted in Islam is the negative power Satan
exerts over all of mankind. But he is not sovereign. Allah alone
carries that distinction. So no matter if Satan tempts and
harasses, the believer may at all times submit to the higher
authority of God and thus secure freedom from all that is evil
and corrupt.

Narrated Abu Huraira: The Prophet said, "No child is born but
that Satan touches it when it is born whereupon it starts crying
loudly because of being touched by Satan, except Mary and her
Son" (6:54; 60.54.71).

Islam teaches against the doctrine of original sin. It claims that, from Adam forward, all of the human race is confronted with the choice of good or evil. Free will mixed with predestination is the determination for one's behavior.

Perhaps this Hadith draws a distinction between inheritance and influence. Satan begins his activity of corruption only at the time of birth, not at the moment of conception. The interesting exceptions are Mary and Jesus. Why is Mary included? Jesus is referred to in the Quran as sinless, but this attribute is not ascribed to Mary. What about Muhammad and his parents? It would appear Satan's touch also extended to them.

> Narrated Ibn Umar: The Prophet said, "There will appear earthquakes and afflictions, and they will come out the side of the head of Satan" (2:81; 17.26.147).

As a survivor of a level-seven earthquake, I, too, probe nature and theology in order to assign first cause to such catastrophes. Muhammad felt he had the ultimate answer to the problem of both earthquakes and other trials of life. All find their source from inside the head of Satan. This would seem to be a simple attribution of all that is evil or destructive to the great adversary Satan.

> Narrated Jabir Abdullah: The Prophet said, "When night falls (or when it is evening), stop your children from going out, for the devils spread out at that time. But when an hour of the night has passed, release them and close the doors and mention Allah's Name, for Satan does not open a closed door. Tie the mouth of your water-skin and mention Allah's Name; cover your containers and utensils and mention Allah's Name. Cover them even by placing something across it, and put out your lamps" (7:362; 69.22.527).

This Hadith presents an intensely personalized description of evil. People as well as material items must be protected from Satan and the devils. These evil ones are moving about in the dark seeking to attack and destroy. Children seem to be their special target.

It is interesting to note how devils seem unable to penetrate doors or covered items that have been sealed with the name of Allah. I have noted that my Muslim friends always keep dishes in a protected area at night. Glasses are turned upside down. My theory was that this was done to keep insects from soiling the household items. Now I understand these actions may have had a religious significance as well.

> Narrated Abu Huraira: The Prophet said, "When you hear the crowing of cocks, ask for Allah's Blessings for (their crowing indicates that) they have seen an angel. And when you hear the braying of donkeys, seek refuge with Allah from Satan for (their braying indicates) that they have seen a devil" (4:332; 54.14.522).

This Hadith places chickens on the side of Allah. Their crowing is a sign for the believer. Angels are in the near neighborhood and the Muslim is to beseech Allah for his blessing. Conversely, the donkey is reputed to have seen a devil when he is braying. This indicates danger, and the follower of Allah is to seek spiritual refuge. I wonder what happens when the cock crows and the donkey brays simultaneously.

> Narrated Abu Huraira: The Prophet said, "Yawning is from Satan and if anyone of you yawns, he should check his yawning as much as possible, for if anyone of you (during the act of yawning) should say: 'Ha', Satan will laugh at him" (4:325; 54.10.509).

Many Muslims (as well as Christians) seek to suppress their yawns. It is unlikely that believers in Islam know the connection between their yawn and Satan. One can only speculate as to how satanic activity is linked to a simple bodily function. The devil's smile seems to be a gesture of derision.

> Narrated Abu Qatada: The Prophet said, "A good dream is from Allah, and a bad dream is from Satan. So whoever has seen (in a dream) something he disliked, then he should spit without saliva, thrice on his left and seek refuge with Allah from Satan, for it will not harm him" (9:105; 87.10.124).

It seems safe to ascribe good dreams to Allah and bad ones to Satan. This dichotomy can be applied to most of life's situations. Spitting three times to one's left side is reputed to give the Muslim protection from the effects of a bad dream. In Islam anything relating to the left is usually associated with dishonor.

Dreams are taken seriously among the followers of the Prophet. One of the intriguing aspects of this nocturnal activity relates to the significant number of Muslims who have testified to the Lord, usually dressed in a white robe, appearing to them in a dream. This has led many to become believers in Christ as Lord and Savior.

Narrated Abu Huraira: The Prophet said, "If anyone of you rouses from sleep and performs the ablution, he should wash his nose by putting water in it and then blowing it out thrice, because Satan has stayed in the upper part of his nose all the night."

[Translator's Note: We should believe that Satan actually stays in the upper part of one's nose, though we cannot perceive how, for this is related to the unseen world of which we know nothing except what Allah tells us through His Apostle] (4:328; 54.10.516).

Once again, faith triumphs over rational thought. The Hadith commentator realizes how absurd it sounds to have Satan dwelling in one's nose and then to be able to expel him by ablutions. But the reader is exhorted to exercise pervasive faith in the apostle and his revelation of the will of God. Any other response would be disobedience and a lack of submission to Allah.

Muhammad and the Supernatural

Narrated Aisha: Allah's Apostle said, "O Aisha! This is Gabriel sending his greetings to you." I said, "Peace, and Allah's Mercy be on him (Gabriel). You see what we do not see." (She was addressing Allah's Apostle) (8:175; 74.16.266).

Muhammad declared that he received revelations from Allah mediated through the angel Gabriel. These heavenly visitations were reputed to have come at varying times and circumstances. The only wife of the Prophet who was present at these auspicious moments was Aisha.

In this Hadith, Muhammad passes on the greetings of Gabriel to Aisha. She is somewhat taken aback and comments that the Prophet is capable of seeing that which his disciples cannot visualize. The inference is that God is uniquely communicating his message to Muhammad in an esoteric manner.

Another heavenly encounter has been recorded in the Hadith.

> Narrated Jabir Abdullah: The Prophet said, "While I was walking
> I heard a voice from the sky. I looked up towards the sky, and
> behold! I saw the same Angel who came to me in the Cave of Hira,
> sitting on a chair between the sky and the earth. I was so terrified
> by him that I fell down on the ground" (6:421; 60.325.448).

It is obvious that Gabriel is the one alluded to. This vision of the
angel sitting on a chair suspended in the sky struck terror in
Muhammad's heart. A sense of awe and humility overwhelmed
the Prophet as he cast himself prostrate on the ground in an act
of worship.

It appears that the angels depicted in the theology of Islam are
closely aligned with the biblical view of these supernatural beings.
In both Traditions angels take on human traits and yet are able
to transcend earthly limitations.

> Narrated Abu Huraira: The Prophet said, "Last night a big demon
> from the Jinns came to me and wanted to interrupt my prayers (or
> said something similar) but Allah enabled me to overpower him.
> I wanted to fasten him to one of the pillars of the mosque so that
> all of you could see him in the morning but I remembered the state-
> ment of my brother Solomon (as stated in Quran): 'My Lord! For-
> give me and bestow on me a kingdom such as shall not belong to
> anybody after me'" (38:35). The subnarrator Rauh said, "He (the
> demon) was dismissed humiliated" (1:268; 8.75.450).

The demon in this Tradition is stated to have been among the jinn.
It is consistent to identify him as actually being a jinn as these
creatures of the spirit world take on characteristics of either good
or evil.

The demon sought to negate the effectiveness of the prayers
of the Prophet. Muhammad discerned this and, after a struggle,
was able to subdue the demon. Once again we see the personifi-
cation of evil as the Prophet relates that his desire was to have
secured the demon against the pillar of the mosque "for all to
see." It was not just Muhammad who had the ability to physically
see the adversary of the believers.

The Prophet had the authority both to bind and to dismiss the
demon. In this instance the evil one was humiliated and told to

depart. Forces of antithesis had engaged and the victory went to Muhammad. Stories of this nature are much appreciated within the worldwide community of Muslims.

> Narrated Aisha: "The first child who was born in the Islamic Land (i.e. Medina) amongst the Emigrants, was Abdullah bin Az-Zubair. They brought him to the Prophet. The Prophet took a date, and after chewing it, put its juice in his mouth. So the first thing that went into the child's stomach, was the saliva of the Prophet" (5:169; 58.44.249).

"Islamic land" here refers to the time of the Hijra. Muslim refugees had fled from Mecca to Medina in A.D. 622 and established their new religious settlement. These events took place immediately after their arrival in Medina when the first Muslim child was born.

Transmission of blessing from the Prophet to the infant is occurring in this Hadith. We may pronounce such a rite to be unsanitary and strange. But the early Muslims were delighted to have had the very saliva of their exalted Prophet entering into the body of their child. This was a blessing of great significance. Surely Muhammad regarded himself as having a supernatural unction of empowerment that could be transmitted from his person to others through body fluids.

> Narrated Aisha: The Prophet continued for such and such period imagining that he had sexual relation with his wife, and in fact he had not. One day he said, to me, "O Aisha! Allah has instructed me regarding a matter about which I had asked Him. There came to me two men, one of them sat near my feet and the other near my head. The one near my feet, asked the one near my head (pointing at me), 'What is wrong with this man?' The latter replied, 'He is under the effect of magic.' The first one asked, 'Who has worked magic on him?' The other replied, 'Lubaid bin Asam.' The first one asked, 'What material (did he use?).' The other replied, 'The skin of the pollen of a male date tree with a comb and the hair stuck to it, kept under a stone in the well of Dharwan.'" Then the Prophet went to that well and said, "This is the same well which was shown to me in the dream. The tops of its date palm trees look like the heads of the devils, and its water looks like the Henna (red dye)

infusion." Then the Prophet ordered that those things be taken out (8:56–57; 72.56.89).

There are few recorded instances in the Hadith of Muhammad being cursed. In this Tradition we have the clearest example of evil magic at work in the life of the Prophet.

Muhammad had been concerned about imagining he had performed sex with his wife when actually he had not. Two men came to the Prophet who quickly discerned the negative effects of magic upon him. They were able to identify the perpetrator as well as the material used and even where it was located. The Prophet verified their claims by finding the power objects in a well. He ordered them removed, and the assumption is that the Prophet then came to a proper understanding of the times he had physical relations with his wife. The interesting point for us is that Muhammad could have been cursed in such a manner. Even though he is portrayed as the greatest prophet of all times, still he was vulnerable to the effects of black magic.

> Narrated Abu Huraira that once he was in the company of the Prophet carrying a waterpot for his ablution and for cleaning his private parts. While he was following him carrying it (i.e. the pot), the Prophet said, "Who is this?" He said, "I am Abu Huraira." The Prophet said, "Bring me stones in order to clean my private parts, and do not bring any bones or animal dung." Abu Huraira went on narrating: So I brought some stones, carrying them in the corner of my robe till I put them by his side and went away. When he finished, I walked with him and asked, "What about the bone and the animal dung?" He said, "They are of the food of Jinns. The delegate of Jinns of (the city of) Nasibin came to me—and how nice those Jinns were—and asked me for the remains of the human food. I invoked Allah for them that they would never pass by a bone or animal dung but find food on them" (5:126; 58.31.200).

This Hadith presents a strange interaction between Muhammad and a delegation of jinn who were evidently assigned to a specific city. The Prophet declares them to be "nice" and grants their request for food (found on bones or animal dung). I cannot think of another citation where jinns are said to eat food. They are spirit beings which move about invisibly. Yet here we see them talking with Muhammad and requesting food.

In this section we see the Prophet was a believer in the spirit world and sought to pacify any evil potential or influence it had. Multiplied millions of his followers have followed his example down through the centuries.

It is right for the Christian to engage the Muslim in serious conversation concerning this area of his or her life. We can assure him of protection through the shed blood of Christ. Peace can be presented as a natural consequence of placing one's faith in the Savior. References from the Bible can be quoted that refer to exorcism and healing.

Dreams have been used by the Lord to bring many Muslims to faith in Christ. We should engage in serious prayer, seeking God's intervention in the minds of Muslims while they sleep.

Forces of the spirit world, both good and bad, are real. As Christians, we can affirm this to Muslims. Then we can proceed to build on this commonality by setting forth a biblical presentation of liberation through the greatest of all spirits—even the Holy Spirit.

esus

*A*l-Bukhari has little to say about Jesus. A few important citations, however, should be considered. Muslims are generally ambivalent about Christ. They desire to honor him as they do Abraham or Moses. But they are caught in an emotional bind each time they mention his name. They are well aware that one-third of the human race ascribes (at least nominally) more than prophethood to Jesus; and that most Christians declare Christ to be God himself. Such "blasphemy" cannot be tolerated by Islam. One Hadith seems to directly address this issue:

> Narrated Abu Huraira: The Prophet said, "Whoever dies while still worshipping anything besides Allah as equal with Allah, will enter Hell (Fire)." And I said, "Whoever dies without worshipping anything (set) as a rival to Allah, will enter Paradise" (6:22; 60.22.24).

As Islam teaches Christ is but a human prophet, Muslims therefore understand Christians to be other than monotheistic. This logic leads them to assign such false worshipers to hellfire. But all Muslims will strongly affirm they believe in Jesus. Without such faith, they say, no one can be a true follower of the religion of Islam.

Narrated Abdullah bin Umar: Allah's Apostle said, "I saw myself (in a dream) near the Kaaba last night, and I saw a man with whitish red complexion, the best you may see among men of that complexion having long hair reaching his earlobes which was the best hair of its sort, and he had combed his hair and water was dropping from it, and he was performing the Tawaf [circumambulation] around the Kaaba while he was leaning on two men or on the shoulders of two men. I asked, 'Who is this man?' Somebody replied, '(He is) Messiah, son of Mary'" (9:106-7; 87.11.128).

Mecca is the setting for the dream of Christ being a Muslim and performing the circumambulation around the Kaaba. Jesus is depicted as an old man requiring the assistance of two men as he walked. Muhammad did not recognize him and had to ask who he was. The reference to Messiah is found in the Quran as well as in the Hadith, although few Muslims understand the word *Messiah*. Certainly Islamic scholars do not accept any connotation of divinity in the term.

Narrated Anas: The Prophet said, "Go to Jesus, Allah's Slave, His Apostle and Allah's Word and a Spirit coming from Him" (6:4).

[Translator's Note: This may be understood as the Spirit or Soul of Allah, in fact, it is a soul created by Allah, i.e. Jesus. It was His Word: 'Be,' and it was created like the creation of Adam] (6:4; 60.3.3).

A number of identifications of Jesus are set forth in this passage. "Slave of Allah" is in close harmony with "apostle." Both words are applied to Muhammad as well. They are human terms that indicate subservience to Allah. "Apostle" goes a bit further and refers to a special relationship to God. In both the Quran and New Testament this word applies to the elect few who are uniquely anointed to perform God's tasks.

Jesus being designated as "Allah's Word" presents difficulties to Islam. The term seems to present a unity with God, and the parallel to the first chapter of John's Gospel cannot be missed. There are Muslims, however, who simply say Christ was a conduit of God's Word that was recorded in the Gospels. They see nothing more mystic in the term than what is implicit in this explanation.

How can Jesus be a spirit that has proceeded from Allah? The note indicates "spirit" refers to the soul of Jesus, which was created by God. I cannot think of any similar reference wherein Muhammad is said to be a spirit. All of these words portray a high opinion of Christ.

It is important to understand the context of the following Tradition. Muhammad is experiencing a vision of what will occur on the day of resurrection. On that occasion people will look for an intercessor who will assist them in gaining admission to paradise. They approach Adam, Noah, Abraham, and Moses, all of whom refuse—they even name their sins. Only Jesus does not claim to be a sinner. This prompts the people to move toward Christ.

> Narrated Abu Huraira: The Apostle said, "So they will go to Jesus and say, 'O Jesus! You are Allah's Apostle and His Word which He sent to Mary, and a superior soul created by Him, and you talked to the people while still young in the cradle. Please intercede for us with your Lord. Don't you see in what state we are?' Jesus will say, 'My Lord has today become as angry as He has never been before, nor will ever become hereafter.' Jesus will not mention any sin, but will say, 'Myself! Myself! Myself! Go to someone else; go to Muhammad.'" (6:200–201; 60.178.236).

Once again we see Jesus referred to as "Allah's Apostle" and his "Word." This "superior soul" was even enabled to speak intelligibly to people while he was still in the cradle. But following these superlatives Christ humbly indicates his inability to function as an intercessor. He specifically refers the supplicants to Muhammad, who has assumed this role on other occasions. So, even though Christ is exalted, it is the Prophet who is presented as the greatest spokesperson of Allah.

> Narrated Abu Huraira: The Prophet said, "When any human being is born, Satan touches him at both sides of the body with his two fingers, except Jesus, the son of Mary, whom Satan tried to touch but failed, for he touched the placenta instead" (6:324; 54.10.506).

Satan is depicted as having an immediate influence on the human race at the moment of birth. This comes about as close as possible to the Christian view of original sin. But, interestingly, Islam teaches Jesus was spared this touch of Satan and sin.

Narrated Abu al-Ashari: Allah's Apostle said, "If a person teaches his slave girl good manners properly, educates her properly, and then manumits [frees her] and marries her, he will get a double reward. And if a man believes in Jesus and then believes in me, he will get a double reward" (6:435; 55.43.655).

This most interesting Hadith focuses upon obtaining a double reward from Allah. Slaves were common during Muhammad's day in Arabia, and severe maltreatment was the norm. By contrast, the Prophet frequently exhorted his followers to treat slaves well. So here the double reward goes to the slave owner who graciously prepares the young girl for freedom and then marries her. This same reward is directed toward anyone who places his or her faith in Jesus and Muhammad. Provocatively, it is to be noted that Abraham, Ishmael, or Moses is not mentioned. On the grassroots level, I have found Muslims give more honor to these three prophets than they do to Jesus.

Narrated Abu Huraira: Then Allah's Apostle said, "By Him in Whose Hands my soul is, son of Mary (Jesus) will shortly descend amongst you people (Muslims) as a just ruler and will break the Cross and kill the pig and abolish the Jizya (a tax taken from the non-Muslims, who are in the protection of the Muslim government). Then there will be abundance of money and nobody will accept charitable gifts" (3:233–34; 34.104.425).

This Tradition contains many strange elements. It declares that Jesus will "shortly" descend from heaven. This was stated by Muhammad six hundred years after Christ's resurrection. The time has now extended another fourteen hundred years.

Jesus will appear among the followers of Ishmael as a Muslim and as a just ruler of Muslims. His will be an exalted position. This perhaps is the reward he receives for the enlightenment he has experienced in heaven. He now has become a true follower of Allah through the revelation of the Prophet.

Christ then repudiates the cross. In a dramatic act, one of the great reputed heresies of Christianity is neutralized. The biblical teaching of salvation through the shed blood of Christ on the cross is denied. The conflict of the ages between Islam and Christianity is at last finished. Muslims have broken the power of the cross—and by the hands of Christ himself. To Christians such an act is utterly unthinkable. To Muslims it is an anticipated event of glorious magnitude. I find Muslims everywhere are aware of this teaching.

The next occurrence concerns Christ killing a pig. Islam has consistently taught against eating this unclean animal. Muslims cannot understand why Christians eat pork when "the Bible clearly presents it as a forbidden meat." It is an indication of the importance of this belief that the subject appears in this particular Hadith.

An abundance of money and financial security will also be part of that great day. There is no indication as to how this will be practically achieved.

From this brief overview of the few Traditions that relate to Christ, the reader will understand that Islam cannot easily just release Jesus into historical irrelevance. He is a continuing force to be reckoned with by laypeople and scholars of Islam throughout the world. But these citations undercut the work of the cross and Christ's salvific ministry to the human race. That is a serious attack on the absolute core of the Christian faith.

Perhaps, most helpful for us is Jesus' being called "Allah's Word." This clear Hadith statement confirms what some Muslim scholars deny is found in the Quran. John 1 will build on this pregnant term and lead to a fuller explanation of Christ's deity.

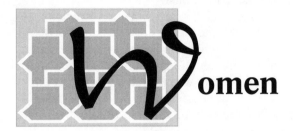

omen

*I*n the eyes of much of the world, Islam is vulnerable to the charge of the abuse of women. Muslims are reported to:

keep their women sequestered in homes or insist they wear complete veils when they go out in public.

practice the dowry system of paying for a wife.

marry a wife when she is very young, usually giving the girl no voice in the selection of her spouse.

give no real opportunity for the wife to initiate divorce proceedings.

invoke the Quran as permission to beat one's wife if she is rebellious.

marry up to four wives at a time, although a woman is allowed to have but one husband.

give a woman's legal voice in a court proceeding the worth of but half that of a man.

allow for little professional development of women in the public sector.

Throughout my career among Muslims in Asia, I have observed illustrations of each point. There can be no dispute as to the reality of abuse directed toward Muslim women. But for each point there is an Islamic response. As I seek to fairly and objectively analyze male-female relationships within the broad communities of Islam and Christianity, I must ask whether either group of people has much about which to boast.

Perhaps only 5 percent of either Muslims or Christians sincerely and fervently follow the teachings of their professed religion. Our evaluations are often based on the 95 percent of nominal adherents of each group, evaluations that result in unbalanced critiques. True, Western Christian women have more freedom in life, but much of this freedom has been gained only in this century. In the United States, the right to vote was obtained through a constitutional amendment passed in 1920.

However, it is my conviction that the Bible sets the stage for equal rights for women much better than do the Quran and Hadith. The reader can consider the information in these next pages and then draw his or her own conclusion.

Standards of Sexual Conduct

Narrated Ibn Abbas: The Prophet said, "Allah has written for Adam's son his share of adultery which he commits inevitably. The adultery of the eyes is the sight (to gaze at a forbidden thing) and the adultery of the tongue is talk. The innermost wishes and desires and the private parts testify to all this or deny it" (8:172; 74.12.260).

Is Allah responsible for foreordaining the inevitability of men committing adultery? This Hadith seems to give such a teaching. The phrase *Allah has written* refers to the predestining activity of God.

Narrated Abu Huraira: The Prophet said, "Seven people will be shaded by Allah under His shade on the day when there will be no shade except His. They are:

. . . 5. A man who refuses the call of a charming woman of noble birth for an illicit sexual intercourse with her and says: 'I am afraid of Allah'" (2:289; 24.15.504).

Prostitution is uniformly denounced in all Islamic Scriptures, as is what can be termed any type of illicit sexual relationship.

Sex with anyone other than one's wife is forbidden (the exception is sex with slaves, which will be discussed later in this chapter). In this Tradition a Muslim is confronted with an alluring sexual temptation. His response is exemplary. The fear of God causes him to refuse an offer that would lead to his defilement.

Dr. Ali has confided to me that several women have attempted to seduce him during his journeys abroad. He told me of his emphatic refusal to engage in such acts that would betray his relationship to Allah and his family. The women could not understand such a commitment to God on the part of a layman. The fear of Allah was and is a present reality within his spiritual grid.

> Narrated Ibn Abbas: The Prophet said, "It is not permissible for a man to be alone with a woman, and no lady should travel except with a Muhram (i.e. her husband or a person whom she cannot marry)" (4:154; 52.140.250).

A very high standard of moral conduct is prescribed in these words. A man is to strictly avoid temptation by refusing to be alone with a woman. Although this may seem an impossible standard in the modern world, I am reminded of Billy Graham. He has successfully avoided even a hint of sexual misconduct in his long successful career by following precisely this code of personal behavior.

> Narrated Abdullah bin Abbas: The Prophet stopped to give the people verdicts. In the meantime, a beautiful woman from the tribe of Khatham came, asking the verdict of Allah's Apostle. Al-Fadl started looking at her as her beauty attracted him. The Prophet looked behind while Al-Fadl was looking at her; so the Prophet held out his hand backwards and caught the chin of Al-Fadl and turned his face (to the other side) in order that he should not gaze at her (8:162; 74.2.247).

Lust, for men, begins with a look or a mental sexual fantasy. From there the temptation can proceed into physical relationship. Muhammad's moral assistance to Al-Fadl was to physically avert his friend's gaze away from the beautiful woman.

Two Hadith cause me to wonder if the Prophet was able to maintain these high moral standards in his own life.

Anas bin Malik said, "Any of the female slaves of Medina could take hold of the hand of Allah's Apostle and take him wherever she wished" (8:62; 72.61.97).

These words can be understood only in the context of early Muslim warriors receiving female slaves as a bounty of war. The conquerors had total rights over these women, including sexual privileges. They were in a different category than were women of the soldier's own tribe.

In this Hadith we find openness between Muhammad and these girls that is prohibited in other settings. These slaves were evidently quite free in their behavior among Muslim men. This Tradition indicates Muhammad enjoyed their attention.

Narrated Anas bin Malik: Allah's Apostle used to visit Um Haram bint Milhan and she was the wife of Ubada bin As-Samit. One day the Prophet visited her and she provided him with food and started looking for lice in his head. Then Allah's Apostle slept. . . .

[Translator's Note: The Prophet was very clean as he used to take a bath daily. It is not logical that he could have had lice in his head. Searching for lice does not necessarily mean that there were any] (9:108; 87.12.130).

A number of questions arise in regard to the Prophet's behavior as set forth in this Hadith. Why did Muhammad repeatedly visit this married woman? There is no indication he went to see her husband, whose name is given only incidentally. The relationship was close enough that the woman fed the Prophet. Intimacy then proceeds to the point where the woman searches through the Prophet's hair in pursuit of any lice that may have taken up residence. During this time he falls asleep. This familiarity seems to exceed the boundaries of decorum set by Muhammad himself.

The note at the conclusion of this Tradition does not focus on the propriety of the Prophet's actions. Rather it digresses into a defense of Muhammad's bathing habits and subsequent cleanness of body. I am not too surprised at this shift of emphasis. Muslims are often so taken up with the minutia of ritual that they miss some of the larger issues of life. This next section addresses some of these areas.

Regulations about Marriage and Divorce

> Narrated Abu Huraira: The Prophet said, "A matron should not be given in marriage except after consulting her; and a virgin should not be given in marriage except after her permission." The people asked, "O Allah's Apostle! How can we know her permission?" He said, "Her silence (indicates her permission)" (7:51–52; 62.42.67).

This Hadith sets forth an ideal that is not generally followed in most of the Islamic world. Young brides-to-be in many Muslim countries simply acquiesce to that which has been arranged by parents or friends. They may well not meet their spouse prior to the wedding day. I have noted this happening among rural and urban Muslims, among the poor and rich. The trend, however, in Islamic societies affected by modernism and secularism is for Muslim girls to have a definite part in the choice.

> Narrated Abu Huraira: The Prophet said, "If a husband calls his wife to his bed (i.e. to have sexual relations) and she refuses and causes him to sleep in anger, the angels will curse her till morning" (4:302; 54.6.640).

As is usual in the Quran and Hadith, the greater concern is for the comfort and preference of the male. There is no list of acceptable reasons that the wife may give for her refusal to have sex with her husband. Rather, the Tradition simply sets forth the duty of the wife and the curse of God that will come upon her if she refuses to obey her husband.

> Al-Hasan and Qatada said regarding a Magian couple who embraced Islam: Their marriage remains valid, but if one of them becomes a Muslim and the other refuses to become a Muslim, the wife is regarded as divorced, and the husband has no right to keep her as a wife (7:158; 63.20.210).

The assumption is that the husband becomes a Muslim and the wife refuses to convert. She then is to be divorced. Muslim men are allowed to be married to women who are Christians, but Muslim women are not to marry Christian men. But this Hadith seems to be addressing the issue of a pagan wife who will not convert to Islam. Thus her marital rights are to be terminated.

> Narrated Abu Huraira: The Prophet said, "It is not lawful for a woman (at the time of wedding) to ask for the divorce of her sister (i.e. the other wife of her would be husband) in order to have everything for herself, for she will take only what has been written for her" (7:62; 62.54.82).

Present wives of Muslim men are to be protected from the greed of younger wives. The new wife is to be party to an agreement regarding what she will receive from her husband. She is to make no further demands. In practice, however, the introduction of a younger, prettier wife usually creates massive dissonance in the home. The husband almost inevitably favors the newest addition. This then is a great opportunity for the most recent wife to gain material goods in a way that generates jealousy among the other wives. I have never had Muslim polygamists testify to me of marital harmony in their homes. Conversely, they have stated how difficult it is to create a climate of love and trust within the family. This problem notwithstanding, the affluent in Islam continue with multiple marriages. As a teacher of Islam with three wives has told me, "God has made this provision for those of us who have sexual needs of a new wife every ten years. This is much better than being like a Christian televangelist who went to prostitutes to fill his physical desires."

> Narrated Aisha: A man may dislike his wife and intend to divorce her, so she says to him, "I give up my rights, so do not divorce me" (3:378; 43.12.630).

Many Muslim women live in fear of divorce. Such a traumatic, life-altering event can be initiated if not finalized (in certain Muslim countries) when the husband simply states, "I divorce you" three times. Disgrace and failure immediately become an integral part of the woman's life. Societal blame usually falls upon her. It is concluded she has some fault or inadequacy that made her displeasing to her husband. She then has a choice to go back to her parents' home or try to survive on her own. She can marry again, but her worth has so diminished in the eyes of men that she will often have to settle for an inadequate husband who has had a problem getting a virgin bride. Islamic society prefers that all women be married. Thus relatives try very hard to arrange another marriage for a divorced wife.

Women thus will endure great abuse in order to remain married. In this Tradition we see a wife's willingness to forego her legitimate rights in order to avoid divorce and the stigma it will bring. She also will be prone to acquiesce to her husband's taking on additional wives so she will not be cast out of the home. It is my observation that this scenario works out more frequently than does divorce.

In the West the divorce rate is said to be in excess of 40 percent. My estimate is that divorce and wife abandonment among Muslims would be less than 15 percent. Girls, from very young ages, are taught that submission to a husband is an imperative. The wife's whole focus in life then becomes pleasing her husband. In this context, men do not feel the need to divorce as readily as do their Western counterparts.

> Narrated Aisha: A man divorced his wife and she married another man who proved to be impotent and divorced her. Then she came to the Prophet and said, "O Allah's Apostle! My first husband divorced me and then I married another man who entered upon me to consummate his marriage but he proved to be impotent and did not approach me except once during which he benefited nothing from me. Can I remarry my first husband in this case?" Allah's Apostle said, "It is unlawful to marry your first husband till the other husband consummates his marriage with you" (7:139; 63.7.190).

This rather strange Hadith remains unexplained. Why is the wife prohibited from remarrying her first husband? Her second husband was impotent and divorced her. Yet the Prophet insists that the second husband have a successful sexual relationship with the woman before a divorce can take place. He is requiring the impossible. As is often the case in complicated Hadith, there is no accompanying explanation that would help us unravel the mystery.

Narrated Uqba bin Al-Harith: I married a woman and then a black lady came to us and said, "I have suckled you both (you and your wife)." So I came to the Prophet and said, "I married so-and-so and then a black lady came to us and said to me, 'I have suckled both of you.' But I think she is a liar." The Prophet turned his face away from me and I moved to face his face, and said, "She is a liar." The Prophet said, "How (can you keep her as your wife when that lady has said that she has suckled both of you? So abandon (i.e. divorce) her (your wife)" (7:28; 62.24.41).

If a mother had problems in breast-feeding her child, it was common to enlist a wet nurse. There would be situations where a woman would be giving her breast milk to infants of a number of different parents. In this Tradition a husband and wife have been told by a wet nurse that she suckled both of them as babies. The husband, in great despair, went to the Prophet and declared the black woman to be a liar. Muhammad ordered this distraught man to divorce his wife, regardless of the truth or otherwise of the woman's claim. Just the charge would be serious enough to justify the radical act of divorce.

This practice is common among Muslims today. No man and woman may marry who have been breast-fed by the same person. Implications of incest seem to be at the root of such a prohibition. I have heard my Muslim friends making a marriage arrangement for their children, emphasizing that the two parties could never have been nursed by the same woman. This Hadith lives on.

Ibn Umar said, "If a slave-girl who is suitable to have sexual relations is given to somebody as a gift, or sold or manumitted (freed), her master should not have sexual intercourse with her before she gets one menstruation so as to be sure of absence of pregnancy, and there is no such necessity for a virgin."
Ata said, "There is no harm in fondling with one's pregnant slave-girl without having sexual intercourse with her" (3:239–40; 34.113.436).

Slaves are property. Therefore, masters (owners) have sexual rights without restriction as to number of slaves or frequency of intercourse. If the girl is pregnant then sexual guidelines are given. Although this seems morally promiscuous, one must remember similar rights were given in the Old Testament to victorious warriors. They were allowed to take the young girls of a defeated tribe as slaves or concubines.

> Narrated Um Salama: Um Sulaim came to Allah's Apostle! and said, "O Allah's Apostle! Verily, Allah does not feel shy to tell the truth. If a woman gets a nocturnal sexual discharge (had a wet dream), is it essential for her to take a bath?" He replied, "Yes, if she notices a discharge" (8:90; 72.79.142).

Once again the meticulous nature of Islamic legalism is highlighted. My view of this Hadith is not that it is a command regarding personal hygiene; rather it refers to a bodily cleansing with implications of a spiritual nature. This bath purifies the woman for prayers or any other religious exercise such as touching the Quran or entering a mosque.

> Narrated Abdullah bin Zama: The Prophet said: "None of you should flog his wife as he flogs a slave and then have sexual intercourse with her in the last part of the day" (7:100–101; 62.94.132).

It is permissible to beat one's wife if she is rebellious. Surah 4:34 states, *"As for those from whom ye fear rebellion, admonish them and banish them to beds apart and scourge them."* So this Hadith does not prohibit flogging one's wife. Rather the husband should refrain from sex with his wife at the end of the day in which he beat her.

> Narrated Alqama: Abdullah (bin Masud) said, "Allah curses those ladies who practise tattooing and those who get themselves tattooed, and those ladies who remove the hair from their faces and those who make artificial spaces between their teeth in order to look more beautiful whereby they change Allah's creation" (6:380; 60.298.408).

There is some difficulty encountered in making an exegesis of this passage. There are a number of specific prohibitions. It is hard to evaluate whether these are all followed. I have never heard of a Muslim woman who was tattooed. The outsider is not privy as to whether Muslim women remove facial hair or create artificial spaces between their teeth. Western women, in contradistinction to this Hadith, often wear braces in order to close gaps between teeth.

The question that arises from this Tradition is whether Muslim women should refrain from doing anything that makes them look more beautiful. If they do make changes, is this really a threat to Allah's creative act? Are the women introducing physical change that is prohibited by Allah? What are the perimeters to these alterations?

My observation is that Muslim women, according to financial ability, do make abundant use of cosmetics, perfumes, deodorants, earrings, necklaces, rings, and exquisite clothing. There can be no doubt the rationale behind these additions to the physical body is to appear and smell more beautiful. The husbands appear to heartily approve. Does this incur the displeasure of Allah?

> Narrated Ibn Abbas: The Prophet said, "If anyone of you on having sexual relations with his wife said (and he must say it before starting) 'In the name of Allah, O Allah! Protect us from Satan and also protect what you bestow upon us (i.e. the coming offspring) from Satan,' and if it is destined that they should have a child then, Satan will never be able to harm that offspring" (1:105; 4.8.143).

The prayer of intent is important in Islamic spirituality. Prior to having sex, the petition for protection against Satan's activity is to be uttered by the husband. This prayer is said to keep Satan from harming any child born to this devout father. I rather doubt that this formula is followed except by a small minority of extremely religious husbands.

> Narrated Ibn Muhairiz: I entered the Mosque and saw Abu Said Al-Khudri and sat beside him and asked him about Al-Azl (i.e. coitus interruptus [interrupted intercourse]). Abu Said said, "We went out with Allah's Apostle for the Ghazwa of Banu Al-Mustaliq and we received captives from among the Arabs and we desired women. Celibacy became hard on us and we loved to do coitus interruptus. So when we intended to do coitus interruptus, we said, 'How can we do coitus interruptus before asking Allah's Apostle who is present among us?' We asked (him) about it and he said, 'It is better for you not to do so, for if any soul till the Day of Resurrection is predestined to exist, it will exist'" (5:317; 59.31.459).

Once again we read of allowing Muslim warriors to have sex with the Arab captive women. There is no question about the morality of this act within the Hadith. The issue raised here regards the interruption of intercourse in order to insure the woman does not get pregnant. Muhammad advises full intercourse, leaving the issue of pregnancy to be resolved by God's sovereign will.

This Hadith supports the serious reservation many Islamic theologians have toward the use of any means of birth control. They strongly feel any such protection is man's interference with the domain of the God who alone can give life. Therefore Islamic majority countries are in conflict between the pragmatics of runaway population growth and the shrill voices of the theologians who feel Allah has spoken definitively on the issue.

The next subject to be considered is most controversial. I will give three distinct Traditions that refer to this topic.

Narrated Jabir bin Abdullah and Salama bin Al-Akwa: While we were in an army, Allah's Apostle said, "If a man and a woman agree (to marry temporarily), their marriage should last for three nights, and if they like to continue, they can do so; and if they want to separate, then they can do so" (7:37; 62.32.52).

Narrated Abdullah: We used to participate in the holy wars carried on by the Prophet and we had no women (wives) with us. So we said (to the Prophet), "Shall we castrate ourselves?" But the Prophet forbade us to do that and thenceforth he allowed us to marry a woman (temporarily) by giving her even a garment, and then he recited (a verse from the Quran):

"O you who believe! Do not make unlawful the good things which Allah has made lawful for you."

[Translator's Note: Temporary marriage (Muta) was allowed in the early days of Islam, but later, at the time of the Khaibar Battle, it was prohibited] (6:110; 60.107.139).

Ali said, "Allah's Apostle forbade the Muta marriage on the Day of the battle of Khaibar." (9:76; 86.4.91).

Since temporary marriage is vigorously condoned by the 10 percent of Muslims who are Shiites, it is proper to quote the late Ayatollah Khomeini, who is still the acknowledged spiritual head of the community.

> A woman may legally belong to a man in one of two ways; by continuing marriage or temporary marriage. In the former, the duration of the marriage need not be specified; in the latter, it must be stipulated, for example, that it is for a period of an hour, a day, a month, a year, or more (Khomeini 1980, 94).

Most Sunni Muslims (90 percent of the worldwide Islamic community) believe temporary marriage was allowed only for a very brief time and was limited to the time of religious battles that required men to be absent from their wives for extended periods of time. They look with disdain on their Shiite Muslim brothers who advocate such promiscuity in these modern times. As is clear from Khomeini's words, this practice is to be considered currently appropriate and may be utilized for a period as short as an hour or as long as a year or more. Khomeini does not restrict such a marriage to times of warfare.

The Hadith quotes Muhammad as allowing temporary marriage for a minimum of three nights with the option of making the relationship permanent. A gift—as little as a garment—should be given to the woman. The Prophet then went further and gave Quranic authentication by applying a verse to temporary marriage that indicates Allah has made the practice fall into the category of a "good thing" that is lawful. Once this clear interpretation has been made by Muhammad himself, it is hard to see how it can be rescinded.

But a further Tradition seems to do just that. Islamic jurists argue over whether *muta* was prohibited for the duration of the battle of Khaibar or was disallowed on a permanent basis. However one views this dilemma, the context seems to always identify the practice with warriors engaged in holy war. It was not to be an everyday practice as Khomeini permits in his writings.

The sad reality is that muta looks like sanctioned prostitution. If one follows Khomeini's clear teaching, a Muslim man and woman may enter into an agreement for sex under the guise of a temporary marriage that can last for as brief a time as one hour.

I recently spoke to a young Palestinian Muslim who has lived with two "Christian" girls for a duration of six months each. He condoned his activities by referring to muta. He felt no spiritual conflict. In fact, he is looking for another girl with whom he can enter into an agreement for a temporary marriage. I want to explicitly state that such an act is blasphemous to most Muslims in the world.

Miscellaneous Teaching

Islam is constantly on the defensive in regard to its view of women. Muslims are forced to interact with difficult Scriptures and Hadith that seem clearly to downgrade and even denigrate women.

> Narrated Abu Huraira: The Prophet said, "A woman is married for four things, i.e., her wealth, her family status, her beauty, and her religion" (7:18; 62.16.27).

Without denying the value and desirability of any of the four items, one ponders why traits such as character and inner beauty are ignored. With the exception of religion, I would consider this list negotiable and open to subjective evaluation. For most men, myself included, marrying a woman of wealth is a nonissue.

If Muslims literally followed these guidelines throughout the Islamic world, there would be millions of unmarriageable spinsters. The requirement of wealth alone would exempt a vast multitude of Muslim women.

> Narrated Abu Huraira: The Prophet said, "Were it not for Eve, no woman would ever betray her husband" (4:400; 56.22.611).

Islamic theology strongly refutes the doctrine of the transmission of sin through Adam. Each person is said to be totally responsible for his or her own transgression. Does this Hadith postulate that Eve's influence is somehow passed along to all other women who betray their husbands? Or is Eve set forth as a scapegoat in order to lessen the guilt of female sinners?

Narrated Abdullah bin Umar: I heard the Prophet saying, "An evil omen is in three things: The horse, the woman, and the house"

[Translator's Note: Superstition is disliked in Islam, but if one should think that there are things of bad omen, one may find such a bad omen in a horse that is obstinate or not used for Jihad; a woman that is sterile or discontented or impudent; a house that is not spacious or far from a mosque or near a bad neighbor] (4:74; 52.47.110).

How does a woman feel about being told she is an evil omen? In this Hadith she is also placed in a category with horses and houses. The extracanonical note does not soften the impact of the Tradition. It only highlights what a Muslim man finds repulsive about a woman. Is it not legitimate to enquire why sterility is a bad omen? Does a woman have some sin that puts her barrenness in an evil context?

Muslim men have repeatedly told me of the Prophet's purpose of multiple marriages in his old age. He was simply caring for widows or forging alliances with the family of his new wife. They always downplay Muhammad's sexual desires.

Narrated Jabir bin Abdullah: [The Prophet] then asked me, "Have you got married?" I replied in the affirmative. He asked, "A virgin or a matron?" I replied, "I married a matron." The Prophet said, "Why have you not married a virgin, so that you may play with her and she may play with you?" Jabir replied, "I have sisters (young in age) so, I liked to marry a matron who could collect them all and comb their hair and look after them" (3:176; 34.35.310).

In this Hadith the Prophet advocates marriage to a virgin rather than to an older, more mature woman (probably a widow). It would seem his inclination toward a playful virgin was dramatized by his marriage to the very youthful Aisha.

Narrated Aisha: The things which annul the prayers were mentioned before me. They said, "Prayer is annulled by a dog, a donkey and a woman (if they pass in front of the praying people)." I said, "You have made us (i.e. women) dogs" (1:291; 9.13.490).

Aisha was certainly a feisty person. She took great exception to being compared with dogs and donkeys, which in themselves are unclean and therefore violate the sanctity of the prayer area. Women present a slightly different problem. Men pray with their eyes open and are therefore cognizant of what is before them. If they are distracted by women they may well be enticed to enter into an act of lust, thereby negating the value of their prayer.

> Narrated Abu Al-Khudri: Once Allah's Apostle went out to the Musalla (to offer the prayer) of Al-Fitr prayer. Then he passed by the women and said, "O women! Give alms, as I have seen that the majority of the dwellers of Hell-fire were you (women)." They asked, "Why is it so, O Allah's Apostle?" He replied, "You curse frequently and are ungrateful to your husbands. I have not seen anyone more deficient in intelligence and religion than you. A cautious sensible man could be led astray by some of you." The women asked, "O Allah's Apostle! What is deficient in our intelligence and religion?" He said, "Is not the evidence of two women equal to the witness of one man?" They replied in the affirmative. He said, "This is the deficiency in your intelligence. Isn't it true that a woman can neither pray nor fast during her menses?" The women replied in the affirmative. He said, "This is the deficiency in your religion" (1:181–82; 6.8.301).

I briefly alluded to an abbreviation of this Hadith in the chapter on hell. Here the Prophet further explains why the majority of the dwellers of hell are women. They are there because of their lack of intelligence—evidenced by the fact that their testimony in a court of law is only worth half of that of a man. In religious matters they are deficient because they cannot pray or keep the fast during the time of their monthly period. They are also declared worthy of hell because of their cursing and ingratitude to their husbands.

Is Muhammad making the point that women are born stupid? Perhaps among his female acquaintances the women were not as intelligent as the men. But what chance did they have in a society that did not give them opportunities for education and self-improvement? Their whole lives were of a servile nature. Caring for husband and children was their total focus of life.

As previously mentioned, women are regarded in Islam as being spiritually unclean during their menstruation. The Hadith then goes on to link this deficiency with a religious inadequacy that restricts them from prayer and fasting. The restriction in turn contributes to the fact that many of them will go to hell.

This whole discussion is rather ludicrous. It seems to me it could only make sense to a very chauvinistic society of self-centered males.

> Al Hasan bin Salih said, "I saw a neighbour of mine who became a grandmother at the age of twenty-one."
>
> [Translator's Note: This woman attained puberty at the age of nine and married to give birth to a daughter at ten; the daughter had the same experience] (3:514; 48.18.831).

This sequence of marriage and birth at such an early age is not promoted. It is merely recorded. But there is no hint in any Hadith that this is wrong. Yet, it must be asked, what girl is emotionally or physically prepared for motherhood at the age of ten?

I must admit my disappointment in the Hadith of this chapter. It is my conviction that a basis of ill treatment of many Muslim women is to be found in these Traditions. How I long for Islamic scholars to find a way to exegete their holy books in such a way as to better provide respect and care for over half of their constituency.

We, as Christians, can share our concerns with Muslims, but we must be careful not to do so with any sense of smug superiority. Our own inadequacies are all too apparent in movies, books, and magazines that degrade women.

17

*M*uhammad's Wives

*F*aithful and devout Muslims vociferously defend the right of the Prophet to have as many wives as he desired. The Quran itself does not limit his number of wives, whereas it stipulates his followers are to have no more than four at any one time. Only once have I heard secular Muslims joke about the sexual powers of the Prophet. If these casual yet profane words were overheard by a religious leader, the penalty in a number of Muslim countries would be death. Salman Rushdie, in his novel *The Satanic Verses*, assigned to prostitutes the names of the wives of Muhammad. My prediction is the death sentence imposed on him for this and other indiscretions in his book will never be reversed. He will pay for his words until he dies or is assassinated.

The Hadith elucidates the interaction the Prophet experienced with his wives. Muslims will not deny or query any of the citations in this chapter. These verses are authoritative records of happenings in the marital life of Muhammad.

Narrated Said bin Jubair: Ibn Abbas asked me, "Are you married?" I replied, "No." He said, "Marry, for the best person of this (Mus-

lim) nation (i.e. Muhammad) of all other Muslims, had the largest
number of wives" (7:5; 42.4.7).

Muslims consider it very important to be married. A single man
or woman over thirty-five years old is considered a serious anomaly. The usual age for marriage, of course, is much younger,
depending on the societal norms of each country.

In the preceding Hadith, the Prophet is presented as a model.
He among Muslims had the greatest number of wives. It is generally believed Muhammad had twelve different spouses. I have
had Muslims express to me their disappointment that Jesus was
not married and therefore did not experience all of life's cycles
as did Muhammad.

> Narrated Anas: The Muslims said amongst themselves, "Will she
> (i.e. Safiya) be one of the mothers of the believers (i.e. one of the
> wives of the Prophet) or just (a lady captive) of what his right hand
> possesses?" Some of them said, "If the Prophet makes her observe
> the veil, then she will be one of the mothers of the believers (i.e.
> one of the Prophet's wives), and if he does not make her observe
> the veil, then she will be his lady slave." So when he departed, he
> made a place for her behind him (on his camel) and made her
> observe the veil (5:371; 59.37.524).

I included this Hadith to point out that Muhammad had female
captives in addition to his twelve wives. As sexual rights came
with the possession of the captives, it is assumed that the Prophet
accepted these physical privileges.

An indication of Muhammad's sex life is seen in this Tradition:

> Narrated Qatada: Anas bin Malik said, The Prophet used to visit
> all his wives in a round, during the day and night and they were
> eleven in number. I asked Anas, "Had the Prophet the strength for
> it?" Anas replied, "We used to say that the Prophet was given the
> strength of thirty (men)" (1:165; 5.13.268).

It is difficult for the monogamous Western Christian to comprehend these facts. But it is equally perplexing for us to realize
that many of the Old Testament prophets had multiple wives.
Solomon possessed seven hundred wives and three hundred con-

cubines. David with his many wives and concubines was still a man after God's heart and was highly commended by the Lord.

> Narrated Sahl: A woman came to the Prophet and said, "I have come to present myself to you (for marriage)." She kept standing for a long period during which period the Prophet looked at her carefully (7:504; 72.49.760).

This Hadith presents a somewhat surprising scenario wherein a woman initiates an attempt to marry the Prophet. It seems Muhammad considered at least her beauty as he gazed upon her for an extended period of time. Another record reveals the Prophet refused the lady's offer of marriage, which confirms that the man had the final say in regard to the choice of a lifetime partner.

> Narrated Anas: When Allah's Apostle married Zainab bint Jahsh, he made the people eat meat and bread to their fill (by giving a banquet). Then he went out to the dwelling places of the mothers of the believers (his wives) as he used to do in the morning of his marriage. He would greet them and invoke good on them, and they (too) would return his greeting and invoke good on him (6:299–300; 60.241.317).

This Tradition reveals a kind of good-natured camaraderie between Muhammad and his wives. On the day of taking a new bride he would greet his wives and they in return would bless him. From this Hadith alone one would not imagine there was any intrigue or jealousy among the Prophet's wives. That actually is far from the true situation.

> Umar then reported how he once put on his outer garment and went to Hafsa and said to her, "O my daughter! Do you argue with Allah's Apostle so that he remains angry the whole day?" Hafsa said, "By Allah, we argue with him." Umar said, "Know that I warn you of Allah's punishment and the anger of Allah's Apostle, O my daughter! Don't be betrayed by the one who is proud of her beauty because of the love of Allah's Apostle for her (i.e. Aisha)" (6:406; 60.316.435).

Apparently Aisha would from time to time promote argu-
mentation with Muhammad. The other wives would join in, with
the alienation lasting for a full day. This greatly disturbed Umar,
whose daughter was also a wife of the Prophet. He placed the
blame on Aisha, whom he regarded as a young girl made vain by
her beauty and proud by Muhammad's special affection for her.

> Narrated Aisha that the Prophet married her when she was six
> years old and he consummated his marriage when she was nine
> years old, and then she remained with him for nine years (i.e., till
> his death) (7:50; 62.39.64).

Muhammad was over fifty years old when he married six-year-
old Aisha. Three years later he commenced having sex with her.
Muslim apologists assure us Aisha had her first period at nine
years of age. Otherwise the marriage would not have been con-
summated while Aisha was so young. This relationship continued until the Prophet died when Aisha was eighteen years old.

> Narrated Abu Musa: Allah's Apostle said, "Many amongst men
> reached (the level of) perfection but none amongst the women
> reached this level except Aisha, Pharaoh's wife, and Mary, the
> daughter of Imran. And no doubt, the superiority of Aisha to other
> women is like the superiority of Tharid (i.e. a meat and bread dish)
> to other meals" (4:411; 55.28.623).

Muhammad is clearly stating that Aisha is superior to his other
wives. According to the Quran a man is to regard all of his wives
as equal. There should be no partiality shown to any of the
spouses. Various Hadith, however, definitely indicate Aisha was
the Prophet's most favored and beloved wife.

> Narrated Urwa: [The Prophet] then said to [Um Salama], "Do not
> hurt me regarding Aisha, as the Divine Inspiration do not come
> to me on any of the beds except that of Aisha." On that Um Salama
> said, "I repent to Allah for hurting you." Then the group of Um
> Salama called Fatima, the daughter of Allah's Apostle, and sent
> her to Allah's Apostle to say to him, "Your wives request you to
> treat them and the daughter of Abu Bakr on equal terms." Then
> Fatima conveyed the message to him. The Prophet said, "O my
> daughter! Don't you love whom I love?" She replied in the affir-

mative and returned and told them of the situation. They requested
her to go to him again but she refused. They then sent Zainab bint
Jahah who went to him and used harsh words saying, "Your wives
request you to treat them and the daughter of Ibn Abu Quhafa on
equal terms." On that she raised her voice and abused Aisha to her
face so much so that Allah's Apostle looked at Aisha to see whether
she would retort. Aisha started replying to Zainab till she silenced
her. The Prophet then looked at Aisha and said, "She is really the
daughter of Abu Bakr" (3:455–56; 47.8.755).

The Prophet is pleading for understanding among his wives.
They are jealous and upset over his obvious preference for Aisha.
Several emissaries were sent to Muhammad requesting him to be
more equitable in his display of affections. His response was
twofold. He first indicated Allah was more inclined toward Aisha
because divine revelation came to him when he was in bed with
her. This did not happen when he was with any of his other wives.
He then asked if they could not love whom he loved. This was
an indirect appeal for the wives to understand and accept his
preference for Aisha. Finally, Zainab went to Muhammad and
Aisha with harsh words of abuse and exhortation, all to no avail.
There is no indication the Prophet was ever willing to lessen his
affection for his teenage lover.

> Narrated Aisha: Allah's Apostle was fond of honey and sweets and
> (it was his habit) that after finishing the Asr prayer he would visit
> his wives and stay with one of them at that time. Once he went to
> Hafsa, the daughter of Umar, and stayed with her more than usual.
> I got jealous and asked the reason for that. I was told that a lady
> of her folk had given her a skin filled with honey as a present, and
> that she made a syrup from it and gave it to the Prophet to drink
> (and that was the reason for the delay) (7:141; 63.8.193).

Jealousy was not a one-way street. Aisha plainly states that she
was envious of the Prophet's spending extra time with another
of his wives.

> Narrated Aisha: When ever Allah's Apostle wanted to go on a jour-
> ney, he would draw lots as to which of his wives would accom-
> pany him. He would take her whose name came out. He used to
> fix for each of them a day and a night. But Sauda bint Zam'a gave

up her (turn) day and night to Aisha, the wife of the Prophet intending to satisfy and please Allah's Apostle by that action (3:462;
47.14.766).

Drawing lots was a common way to resolve dilemmas. Only
one wife would accompany the Prophet on his journey. Selection
by lot determined who among the wives would be privileged to
travel with Muhammad. At least one wife realized the best way
to remain in good stead with the Prophet was to give her turn
over to Aisha. This honor was not given to any of the other wives,
only to favored Aisha.

> Aisha said, "I used to say to him [Muhammad], 'If I could deny
> you the permission (to go to your other wives) I would not allow
> your favour to be bestowed on any other person'" (6:296;
> 60.23.312).

Muhammad was a famous person in Arabia during the time
he was married to Aisha. She felt greatly honored to be the favored
wife of the Prophet of Allah. Yet she could not help but entertain
jealous thoughts toward the other wives who also had sexual privileges with her beloved husband. This was frequently stated to
Muhammad.

Two Hadith relate to Aisha and Muhammad's first wife,
Khadija.

> Narrated Aisha, I did not feel jealous of any of the wives of the
> Prophet as much as I did of Khadija (although) she died before he
> married me, for I often heard him mentioning her, and Allah had
> told him to give her the good tidings that she would have a palace
> of Qasab (i.e. pipes of precious stones and pearls in Paradise), and
> whenever he slaughtered a sheep, he would send her women-
> friends a good share of it (5:103; 58.21.164).

> Narrated Aisha: Once Hala bint Khuwailid, Khadija's sister, asked
> the permission of the Prophet to enter. On that, the Prophet
> remembered the way Khadija used to ask permission, and that
> upset him. He said, "O Allah! Hala!" So I became jealous and said,
> "What makes you remember an old woman amongst the old
> women of Quraish, an old woman (with a toothless mouth) of red

gums who died long ago, and in whose place Allah has given you somebody better than her?" (5:105; 58.21.168).

Khadija was a very special wife to Muhammad. She believed in the Prophet even when he was being discredited by friends and foes alike. He never married anyone else while she was alive. Their relationship seemed exemplary, so much so that Aisha became intensely jealous of a memory. Aisha lashed out at Muhammad: How could he so often think of an old toothless woman who had died so long ago? There is no indication as to what the Prophet responded. But most probably he sought to pacify her without in the least demeaning the memory of his special relationship with Khadija.

> Narrated Aisha: I used to look down upon those ladies who had given themselves to Allah's Apostle and I used to say, "Can a lady give herself (to a man)?" But when Allah revealed:
>
> *You (O Muhammad) can postpone (the turn of) whom you will of them (your wives), and you may receive any of them whom you will; and there is no blame on you if you invite one whose turn you have set aside (temporarily), (Quran 33:51)*
>
> I said to the Prophet, "I feel that your Lord hastens in fulfilling your wishes and desires" (6:295; 60.240.311).

Feisty Aisha once again makes her pertinent point to Muhammad. The Prophet had received a rather earthy revelation concerning his right to sleep with whichever of his wives he desired in the order he chose. Aisha felt that Muhammad was too easily receiving divine direction to authenticate his personal preferences. So she observes that Allah appears to quickly fulfill the wishes of the Prophet. In reality, she indirectly questions whether Muhammad's revelations are a product of his own mind.

Parenthetically, it is interesting to note such a time-bound and highly personalized verse of the Quran. My Muslim friends are always quick to tell me of the majestic and timeless revelations of Allah as found in the Quran. This passage certainly does not seem to meet that criteria.

An important incident occurred in the life of Aisha that was extremely controversial and unsettling. The story is repeated a number of times in the Al-Bukhari collection of Hadith. Here is Aisha's version of that happening.

> Narrated Aisha: Whenever Allah's Apostle intended to go on a journey, he used to draw lots amongst his wives, and Allah's Apostle used to take with him the one on whom the lot fell. He drew lots amongst us during one of the battles which he fought. The lot fell on me and so I proceeded with Allah's Apostle after the revelation (of the Verse) of the Veil. I was carried (on the back of a camel) in my howdah [carriage] and carried down while still in it (when we came to a halt). So we went on till Allah's Apostle had finished from that battle of his and returned. When we approached the city of Medina, he announced at night that it was time for departure. So when they announced the news of departure, I got up and went away from the army camps, and after finishing from the call of nature, I came back to my riding animal. I touched my chest to find that my necklace which was made of Zifar beads (i.e. Yemenite beads partly black and partly white) was missing. So I returned to look for my necklace and my search for it detained me. (In the meantime) the people who used to carry me on my camel, came and took my howdah and put it on the back of my camel on which I used to ride, as they considered that I was in it. In those days women were light in weight for they did not get fat, and flesh did not cover their bodies in abundance as they used to eat but a little food. Those people therefore, disregarded the lightness of the howdah while lifting and carrying it; and at that time I was still a young girl. They made the camel rise and all of them left (along with it). I found my necklace after the army had gone. Then I came to their camping place and found no one who would respond to my call. So I intended to go to the place where I used to stay, thinking that they would miss me and come back to me. While I was sitting in my resting place, I was overwhelmed by sleep and slept. Safwan bin Al-Mu'attal As-Sulami Adh-Dhakwani was behind the army. When he reached my place in the morning, he saw the figure of a sleeping person and he recognized me as he had seen me before the order of compulsory veiling (was prescribed). So I woke up when he recited Istirja (i.e. "Truly to Allah we belong and truly to Him we shall return" (2:156)) as soon as he recognized me. I veiled my face with my head cover at once, and by Allah, we did not speak a single word, and I did not hear him saying any word besides his Istirja. He dismounted from his camel and made it kneel down, putting his leg on its front legs and then I got up and rode on it.

Then he set out leading the camel that was carrying me till we over-
took the army in the extreme heat of midday while they were at a
halt (taking a rest). (Because of the event) some people brought
destruction upon themselves and the one who spread the Ifk (i.e.
slander) most was Abdullah bin Ubai Ibn Salul (5:139–40;
59.33.462).

Word quickly spread that Aisha had spent time alone with a
young soldier. Rumor circulated that she had sex with the man.
Muhammad became extremely upset and ordered Aisha to remain
in her parents' house until he could determine the credibility of
the accusations. Aisha was agitated to think that her husband
could even suspect her of any type of moral indiscretion. She let
him know of her anger at being unjustly accused of wrongdoing.

After some days Muhammad became convinced of Aisha's
innocence. This was the occasion for the revelation of a new
Quranic verse that set forth penalties for the sin of slander. The
Prophet and Aisha were then happily reunited.

> Narrated Aisha: . . . Abu Bakr [Aisha's father] came to me and hit
> me violently on the chest and said, "You have detained the peo-
> ple because of a necklace." I kept as motionless as a dead person
> because of the position of Allah's Apostle (on my lap) although
> Abu Bakr had hurt me (with the slap) (6:105; 60.101.132).

Referring to the same incident, Aisha tells of her father's anger
and punishment for her foolish behavior. A previous Hadith says
Abu Bakr also hit her on her flanks.

> Aisha said, "O my head!" (headache) Allah''s Apostle said, "If that
> (i.e., your death) should happen while I am still alive, I would ask
> Allah to forgive you and would invoke Allah for you." Aisha said,
> "O my life which is going to be lost! By Allah, I think that you wish
> for my death, and if that should happen then you would be busy
> enjoying the company of one of your wives in the last part of that
> day" (9:246; 89.51.324).

Once again we receive an insight into the marital life of
Muhammad. Aisha was continually irritated by having to share
her husband with the other wives. As we see in this Hadith, she

did not hesitate to use cynicism to make her point with Muhammad.

In conclusion, it can be stated that the Prophet was not only a lover and provider for his wives; he also was forced to play the role of an arbiter. There seemed to be a distinct lack of harmony in his family life. But Muslims almost never refer to these negative incidents. They proclaim Muhammad as the ideal husband and father.

egalisms

*T*hroughout this book it has been obvious that Islam places great priority on edicts that tightly regulate the activities of the community of the faithful. These widely observed legalisms promote the homogeneity of Islam. Converts to the Muslim faith often highlight Islam's clarity of religious demands as one of the attractions that drew them to their new allegiance. Conversely, few Caucasians would even consider joining a religion that makes so many demands on its adherents.

This brief chapter presents a few of the more mundane Hadith. These rituals and pronouncements are mandated for the devout.

> Narrated Abu Uqba: The Prophet said, "If you do not feel ashamed do whatever you like" (4:457; 55.46.690).

Shame is an important societal constraint within Islam. Muslims hesitate to perform any act that would bring disrepute upon their family name. So Muhammad here is making an appeal for righteous living in the form of a principle. One's sense of shame is to be conditioned by the teachings of the Quran and Hadith. Therefore any act outside of this perimeter of guidance will bring shame and must be avoided. Other deeds that do not generate shame are permissible.

> Narrated Al-Mughira bin Shuba: The Prophet said, "Allah has forbidden for you (1) to be undutiful to your mothers, (2) to bury your daughters alive, (3) to not pay the rights of others (e.g. charity etc.,) and (4) to beg of men (begging). And Allah has hated for you (1) Vain, useless talk, or that you talk too much about others (2) to ask too many questions (in disputed religious matters) and (3) to waste wealth (by extravagance)" (3:348–49; 41.19.591).

Most of these prohibitions are uncontroversial and as relevant today to Muslims as they were in the seventh century when first uttered by the Prophet. It is true many of the faithful prefer to have sons rather than daughters, but in these days there are few if any instances recorded of Muslims burying their daughters alive. This was more of a pre-Islamic practice that Muhammad was protesting.

> Narrated Sad: A man peeped into the house of the Prophet through a hole while the Prophet was scratching his head with a Midrai (a certain kind of comb). On that the Prophet said (to him), "If I had known that you had been looking, then I would have pierced your eye with that instrument, for asking permission has been ordained so that one would not see things unlawfully" (7:529; 72.75.807).

Privacy seemed to have been a priority to Muhammad. His immense popularity provided him with little solitude. As well, having multiple wives who were experiencing fits of extreme jealousy probably made him want to ensure maximum privacy with each spouse. His pronounced punishment would certainly act as an effective deterrent to any potential offender.

> Narrated Aisha: The Prophet used to like to start from the right side on wearing shoes, combing his hair and cleaning or washing himself and on doing anything else (1:117–18; 4.31.169).

The right side of the body is to be preferred to the left. Most Muslims I have known or observed have followed this example.

There is an almost mystical relationship in Islam between spirituality and the washing of the body. The ablutions preceding prayer are obligatory. Practically speaking, this means the devout Muslim washes his head, arms, hands, and feet five times a day.

But such cleansing does not stop there. Other rituals and prohibitions are to be observed.

> Narrated Uqba bin Sahban: The Prophet forbade the throwing of small stones (with two fingers). Abdullah bin Al-Mughaffal Al-Muzani also said, "The Prophet also forbade urinating at the place where one takes a bath" (6:347; 60.275.365).

In Bangladesh, I noted that in many houses the commode was in an area away from the bathing facility. I surmised this was simply a hygienic measure because of an inadequate drainage system. While this is true, certainly the example of the Prophet is a further incentive to follow this practice.

> Narrated Al-Ansari: Allah's Apostle said, "If anyone of you goes to an open space for answering the call of nature he should neither face nor turn his back towards the Qibla [direction of prayer]; he should either face the east or the west" (1:106; 4.11.146).

In one of the homes we rented, the Muslim owner constructed a commode that he was especially proud of. He, with a flair of religiosity that he really didn't possess, assured us the backside of the person using the facility would never be directed toward Mecca. This, he exclaimed, was precisely the teaching of his exalted Prophet. The Hadith substantiates his concern for directional propriety.

> Narrated Abu Qatada: Allah's Apostle said, "When you urinate, do not touch your penis with your right hand; and when you cleanse yourself after defecation, do not use your right hand" (7:365; 69.25.534).

Left-handed people are almost never found among Muslims. If an infant has such a tendency, he or she is immediately trained (and punished, if necessary) to use the right hand only for writing and giving or receiving items. A handshake must always be done with the right hand. In any of these activities, the use of the left hand would be terribly offensive.

Likewise, care must be maintained to only use the left hand in acts of urination or defecation. The right hand is to be kept maximally clean and ritually pure.

Narrated Anas bin Malik: Whenever Allah's Apostle went to answer the call of nature, I along with another boy used to accompany him with a tumbler full of water. (Hisham commented, "So that he might wash his private parts with it)" (1:109; 4.15.152).

Narrated Abu Huraira: I followed the Prophet while he was going out to answer the call of nature. He used not to look this way or that. So, when I approached near to him he said to me, "Fetch for me some stones for cleaning the private parts (or said something similar), and do not bring a bone or a piece of dung" (1:111; 4.20.157).

Muhammad's preference was to clean himself with water. However, in the desert, this was often an impossibility. So the Prophet would resort to the use of sand or stones. He specifically refused bones or dung for cleaning purposes. In these modern times, it is common to see Muslims carrying a small pot with a spout while on a journey. This is used to facilitate their cleansing.

Muslims consider the use of toilet paper to be extremely unhygienic. It is said to inadequately clean one's body as well as to create a problem of disposal in places where proper sewage facilities are not available. A third problem relates to the high cost of paper, which poor Muslims simply cannot afford. Needless to say, people of olden days did not use toilet paper. In Ephesus we visited a first-century public bathhouse in which commodes were lined up next to one another behind a gutter that had been filled with running water.

Narrated Aisha: I used to wash the traces of Janaba (semen) from the clothes of the Prophet and he used to go for prayers while traces of water were still on it (water spots were still visible) (1:146; 4.68.229).

Over the years, I have always been surprised to find how casually Muslims talk about sex. To them it is a natural and important area of life that, if properly regulated, should bring about no shame or embarrassment as the subject arises in everyday conversation. Aisha illustrates this vividly as she writes of her husband, the great "Messenger of Allah," walking out of the house with overt evidence of his recent sexual activity.

Washing semen from clothes as well as from the body is important to Muslims. At 3 A.M. in the village in which we lived, I heard Muslim men taking a bath at their well adjacent to our bedroom window. Upon arising later that morning I asked my neighbors why they were taking a nocturnal bath. With downcast eyes they muttered some unintelligible words. It would be my opinion that they were probably cleaning up after a session with prostitutes.

Ritual, legalisms, and cleansings are all part of the warp and woof of Islam. To the outsider, they seem restrictive and laborious. To the insider who deeply loves Allah and desires to fully follow the Prophet, they are a joy and delight.

But . . . does the "average Muslim" even begin to keep the multitudes of mandated laws within Islam? Emphatically, no! Therefore, it seems appropriate to use this as a talking point in regard to one's relationship with Allah. Has God set forth a totally unobtainable standard for his creation? Does Allah rejoice in seeing the failures of the human race? Has he not made a better plan for man to be delivered from himself and his own carnal desires?

At this point, one can cite verses in Galatians and Romans that point to the superiority of grace over law. Personal testimony can be given that highlights the mercy of God in one's life. I have often seen this approach touch the mind and heart of a Muslim to whom I was speaking.

19

*F*ood

*I*n order for Islam to fulfill its claim to being a total code of life, it is necessary that the Hadith gives teaching in all areas of social mores. Even such a basic subject as eating habits is to be regulated to some extent by the words and example of the Prophet. A few of these citations are noted in this chapter.

> Narrated, Umar Salama: Allah's Apostle said, "Mention the Name of Allah and eat with your right hand, and eat of the dish what is nearer to you" (7:221; 65.2.288).

The most common manner in which Allah's name is invoked is by saying, "Bismillahar Rahmanar Rahim" (In the name of God, the compassionate, the merciful). This is a norm for many Muslims and is stated at the commencement of eating a meal. Eating with one's right hand is obligatory (see chap. 18). Muslims consider it rude to reach across a table for food. They are to wait until the dish is placed nearby before they partake of its contents. In many Muslim homes the wife or a servant acts as a waitress, standing at the table while placing serving bowls close to those who are eating. That person will then eat at a later time.

Narrated Ibn Abbas: The Prophet said: "When you eat, do not wipe your hands till you lick it or have licked it, or had it licked by somebody else" (7:265; 65.53.366).

It is common for Muslims to lick their fingers after eating a meal. They will then wash their hands and mouth with water. I have never heard of a Muslim having his hands licked by another person. This may have been a social custom in the time of the Prophet.

Narrated Maimuna: A mouse fell into the butter and died. The Prophet was asked about that. He said, "Throw away the mouse and the butter that surrounded it, and eat the rest of the butter" (7:317; 67.34.446).

This Tradition sounds a bit crude to the twentieth-century Westerner. But, in reality, if the dead mouse had been in the butter only for a very brief time, I assume the untouched portion would have been unaffected.

Narrated Abu Huraira: A man used to eat much, but when he embraced Islam, he started eating less. That was mentioned to the Prophet who then said, "A believer eats in one intestine (is satisfied with a little food) and a Kafir [unbeliever] eats in seven intestines (eats much)" (7:233; 65.13.309).

The point of this Hadith seems to be that food occupies lesser prominence in one's life after conversion to Islam. I have not observed that Muslims who have adequate financial resources eat any less than those outside of the Islamic faith.

Narrated Abu Huraira: The Prophet never criticized any food (he was invited to) but he used to eat if he liked the food, and leave it if he disliked it (7:241; 65.22.320).

Although the Prophet did not verbally criticize the food he was offered, he felt free to not eat the portion he disliked. I have found Muslims, unlike Muhammad, to be verbally candid concerning their opinion of food. In some contexts a woman can expect to be slapped if the evening meal does not come up to the expectations of her husband.

> Narrated Abaya bin Raifaa: Allah's Apostle said, "If the instrument
> used for killing causes the animal to bleed profusely and if Allah's
> Name is mentioned on killing it, then eat its meat" (i.e. it is law-
> ful) (4:198; 52.191.309).

The word *halal* indicates that the animal has been properly
and lawfully butchered and is thus declared clean. Allah's name
has been invoked at the moment of slitting the throat and then
the blood is completely expelled from the animal. If these two
conditions have not been met, then the meat is *haram* or unlawful to eat.

An orthodox Muslim is rigorously careful to obey these Islamic
regulations. In addition, he or she will never eat pork. This prohibition supposedly extends to any product made from pig fat
such as lard or even some kinds of soap. A kitchen in which pork
is cooked is declared haram. Some Muslims consider Christians
to be unclean because they eat pork. These are extreme reactions,
not common among rank-and-file Muslims.

> Narrated Aisha: Some people said, "O Allah's Apostle! Meat is
> brought to us by some people and we are not sure whether the
> name of Allah has been mentioned on it or not (at the time of
> slaughtering the animals)." Allah's Apostle said (to them), "Men-
> tion the name of Allah and eat it" (3:156; 34.6.273).

My friend Dr. Ali was deeply concerned about going to Harvard University as a visiting scholar and being placed in a situation where available food was not halal. He approached his imam,
who assured him, on the basis of the preceding Hadith, that he
could simply invoke the name of Allah over the meat and then
proceed to eat it. This, of course, would not apply to pork.

> Az-Zuhri said: There is no harm in eating animals slaughtered by
> Arab Christians. If you hear the one who slaughters the animals
> mentioning other than Allah's Name, don't eat of it, but if you do
> not hear that, then Allah has allowed the eating of animals slaugh-
> tered by them, though he knows their disbelief (7:302; 67.22.415).

In attempting to understand this Hadith it is important to realize all Christian Arabs refer to God as Allah. This was done in
pre-Islamic as well as in Islamic times. So, if the Christian either

slaughters in Allah's name or in no name at all, the food is halal to Muslims. Only if he uses the name of a false god is the food considered to be haram.

This Tradition does make a distinction of the Muslim's faith compared to that of the Christian. The follower of Christ is designated a person of "disbelief." This would refer to his nonacceptance of the basic tenets of Islam. Yet, he is a person of the book, that is, the pre-Islamic Old and New Testament Scriptures. Therefore he is not to be totally rejected.

> Narrated Abu Tha'laba Al-Khushani: I said, "O Allah's Prophet! We are living in a land ruled by the people of the Scripture. Can we take our meals in their utensils? In that land there is plenty of game and I hunt the game with my bow and with my hound. Then what is lawful for me to eat?" He said "As for what you have mentioned about the people of the Scripture, if you can get utensils other than theirs, do not eat out of theirs, but if you cannot get other than theirs, wash their utensils and eat out of it" (7:282; 67.4.387).

Some contemporary Muslims hesitate to eat from utensils that do not belong to people of their own faith. They do not like to accept invitations to non-Muslim homes. Eating in nonhalal restaurants is avoided as much as possible. Their rationale is contained in this Tradition. But such extreme actions are reserved for the legalistic few.

> Narrated Abu Huraira: Allah's Apostle said, "If a dog drinks from the utensil of anyone of you, it is essential to wash it seven times" (1:120; 4.34.173).

Just as a dog can defile a place of worship, so it can also render eating utensils unclean. The sevenfold washing of the bowl brings it back into the halal category. This Hadith presents one more reason why Muslims generally avoid having dogs in their homes.

> Narrated Ibn Umar: Allah's Apostle said, "Whoever drinks alcoholic drinks in the world and does not repent (before dying), will be deprived of it in the Hereafter" (7:338; 69.1.481).

Wine in heaven will be different from that which is found on earth. It will be available in abundance and is reputed to be made of a substance that does not cause drunkenness. It will be one of the delights of heaven that believers are prohibited from pre-empting here on earth.

Proportionate to the Christian community, a much smaller percentage of Muslims drink alcoholic beverages. There is a strong social and theological bias against even social drinking.

> Narrated Ibn Umar: The Prophet said, "There is a tree among the trees which is similar to a Muslim (in goodness), and that is the date palm tree" (7:261; 65.47.359).

In the time of the Prophet, dates formed an important part of the Arabs' diet. Date trees were found abundantly throughout the desert of Arabia. Because of Muhammad's affinity for dates, they have taken on an almost religious significance for Muslims. Especially during the holy month of Ramadan this fruit is found plentifully in bazaars throughout the Islamic world. It is the favorite food for breaking the fast at sunset.

> Narrated Anas bin Malik: Someone came to Allah's Apostle and said, "The donkeys have been eaten (by the Muslims)." The Prophet kept quiet. Then the man came again and said, "The donkeys have been eaten." The Prophet kept quiet. The man came to him the third time and said, "The donkeys have been consumed." On that, the Prophet ordered an announcer to announce to the people, "Allah and His Apostle forbid you to eat the meat of donkeys." Then the cooking pots were upset while the meat was still boiling in them (5:361; 59.37.511).

Pork is a meat forbidden to be eaten by decree of God himself in the Old Testament. The Hadith goes a step further by also declaring donkey meat to be haram.

> Narrated Jabir bin Abdullah: The Prophet said, "Whoever has eaten garlic or onion, should keep away from us, or should keep away from our mosque and should stay at his home" (9:337; 92.24.458).

In certain Muslim majority countries garlic and onions are greatly appreciated additions to food preparation. Both condiments are strong and if used in large quantities could lead to what some may regard as an unpleasing smell on one's breath. The prohibition in this Tradition is unusually severe. One could question how bad breath could defile a place of worship. This can be understood only in light of Islam's heavy emphasis on externals. In practical terms I have never heard this Hadith referred to or enforced.

> Narrated Anas: "To the best of my knowledge, the Prophet did not take his meals in a big tray at all, nor did he ever eat well-baked thin bread, nor did he ever eat at an eating table" (7:227; 65.8.298).

Muslims are expected to emulate the Prophet's habits in all areas of life. This simply doesn't work in regard to this verse. Muslims all over the world love thin baked bread. In an Islamic country like Pakistan it is the very staple of the diet. It would be hard to imagine Pakistanis having a meal without chapatis or nan to accompany their curry.

Many Muslims eat at a table rather than sitting on the floor in Middle Eastern fashion. This Hadith is more descriptive than prescriptive. But it still carries the weight of the Prophet's example.

As among all peoples, food is a central focus of life to the Muslims. However, ethnic and cultural distinctions in varying Islamic communities contribute to a heterogeneous interpretation of these Hadith. A few eating and dietary habits are normative, but most are subject to preferences dictated by millennia of cultural influences. Overall, imams are rather passive about enforcing these precedents and regulations.

edicine

roponents of Hadith are somewhat perplexed as to how to reconcile certain of Al-Bukhari's statements with modern medical practices. They are forced, albeit with great reluctance, to question the validity of blatantly outdated and unscientific Hadith-sanctioned remedies. It is painful for Muslim apologists to admit that the Prophet could have been mistaken in his medical opinions. To have to admit that Muhammad was time- and culture-bound in his knowledge, subject to all the scientific inaccuracies of the seventh century, is extremely difficult for them. The children of Ishmael are obligated to emulate the Prophet in all areas of life. How can they accept false advice?

This chapter will highlight a few of the enigmas confronted by the intelligent, modern reader of Muhammad's words. One can go only so far in defense of some of these Hadith. Some Muslim scholars have pressed themselves beyond credulity. By and large, they simply ignore the more embarrassing Traditions. I remember the look of utter consternation when I asked an imam about Muhammad's advice to drink camel's urine for one's health. He replied, "How did you know about that Hadith? Almost no Muslim knows that is in the Traditions!" It seems that keeping people in ignorance is an effective way to avoid theological embarrassment. This, incidentally, is a modus operandi not altogether unknown to Christian theologians and pastors.

> Narrated Abu Huraira: The Prophet said, "No disease has Allah created but that He has created its treatment" (7:395; 71.1.582).

God is always regarded as first cause according to Muslim belief. Therefore it is no surprise to find the creation of disease attributed to Allah. But the Hadith goes on to state that God also has provided a treatment for every disease known to man. I'm sure medical researchers would appreciate being informed of these cures, especially for AIDS and certain kinds of cancer.

> Narrated Aisha: The Prophet said: "Fever is from the increase in the flames of (Hell) Fire and comes out of its heat; so, cool it with water" (4:314; 54.9.485).

I have observed that many Muslims pour water over the head of a person who has a high fever. This Hadith indicates at least one of the sources of this treatment. More interestingly, we also read that fever emanates from an increase in the heat of hell. Just how literally this is to be interpreted is left to the reader.

> Narrated Um Mihsan: I heard the Prophet saying, "Treat with Indian incense, for it has healing for seven diseases; it is to be sniffed by one having throat trouble, and to be put into one side of the mouth of one suffering from pleurisy" (7:402; 71.10.596).

A number of Hadith highlight the healing properties of incense. Having lived among Muslims in the Indian subcontinent for twenty years, I have not seen them using incense for any purpose other than to appreciate its smell. Never have I heard that incense will heal seven diseases. It seems impossible to imagine anyone putting incense inside his or her mouth to aid in healing pleurisy.

> Narrated Anas: The Prophet said, "The best medicines you may treat yourselves with are cupping [withdrawal of blood] and sea incense." He added, "You should not torture your children by treating tonsillitis by pressing the tonsils or the palate with the finger, but use incense" (7:403–4; 71.13.599).

Throughout the centuries cupping was a standard form of medical treatment. The simple idea was to withdraw diseased blood and then allow the body to replenish the circulatory system with that which is pure. Several Hadith speak of this practice in a positive manner.

> Narrated Ibn Abbas: Once the Prophet got his blood out (medically) and paid that person who had done it. If it had been illegal the Prophet would not have paid him (3:179–80; 34.40.316).

Medicine as a science was in its infancy in the time of Muhammad. He was utilizing the best current medical practice of the day. But, today it is known that cupping a small amount of blood is valuable only for use in testing procedures. There are rare instances when a patient's blood is removed, treated, and then replaced. This is a sophisticated procedure totally unknown and impossible to have been performed in Muhammad's day.

So it is not at all unusual for the Prophet to echo the wisdom of the age. The only problem arises when some of his followers insist on elevating such historical happenings to religious and legalistic edicts applicable to all times and places. Such people find themselves ridiculed by Muslims and non-Muslims alike.

> Narrated Abu Said Al-Khudri: One of them (the Prophet's companions) started reciting Surat-al-Fatiha and gathering his saliva and spitting it (at the snake-bite). The patient got cured . . . (7:424; 71.33.632).

Saliva of an empowered person is a transferable body fluid said to contain healing properties. Jesus and Muhammad used it, as did the Prophet's companions.

> Narrated Aisha: The Prophet used to say to the patient, "In the Name of Allah. The earth of our land and the saliva of one of us may cure our patient."

> [Translator's Note: The Prophet, while reciting the Ruqya [recitation of divine verses as treatment for a disease], put some of his saliva on his index finger and touched the earth with it and applied the resulting mixture to the place of the ailment] (7:429; 71.38.641).

Saliva is used by Muslims for purposes other than healing. Once, while attending a Sufi Muslim gathering, I was privileged to watch an aged *pir* (Sufi holy man) induct a group of one hundred followers into his order. A pitcher of lemonade was placed on a table in front of him. The pir breathed into the pitcher. He put his finger into a glass of lemonade, withdrew his finger, and then placed it in his mouth. He then dipped his finger into the glass. This procedure was repeated three times.

The glass of "empowered" lemonade was poured into the larger pitcher. Assistants then poured out small amounts and gave each of the new initiates a drink. A transmission of power from pir to disciples had supposedly taken place through the medium of human saliva. I am sure the Muslims also gained hope that they might retain good health and live to the pir's ripe old age of 120 years.

Other forms of healing as recorded in the Hadith seem to have a flavor of animism in them.

Narrated Israil: Uthman bin Abdullah bin Mauhab said, "My people sent me with a bowl of water to Um Salama." Israil approximated three fingers (indicating the small size of the container in which there was some hair of the Prophet). Uthman added, "If any person suffered from evil eye or some other disease, he would send a vessel (containing water) to Um Salama. I looked into the container (that held the hair of the Prophet) and saw a few red hairs in it."

[Translator's Note: Um Salama would dip those hairs into the vessel and return it to the patient to drink that blessed water or wash himself with it, seeking to be healed] (7:518; 72.66.784).

This prescription is based on the superstitious belief that healing and protection would be acquired by drinking or being anointed by water that had been blessed through contact with the hairs of Muhammad. Herein lies one more conflict for the theologian. How can hair of a human being be so efficacious? Besides this was at best a temporary provision. How long would the hairs of the Prophet be available? And how far distant from Arabia would they be found?

Narrated Khalid bin Sa'd: We went out and Ghalib bin Abjar was accompanying us. He fell ill on the way and when we arrived at Medina he was still sick. Ibn Abi Atiq came to visit him and said to us, "Treat him with black cumin. Take five or seven seeds and crush them (mix the powder with oil) and drop the resulting mixture into both nostrils, for Aisha has narrated to me that she heard the Prophet saying, 'This black cumin is healing for all diseases except As-Sam.'" Aisha said, "What is As-Sam?" He said, "Death" (7:400; 71.7.591).

I am sure this Hadith would not make pharmaceutical companies happy. Every nonfatal disease is reputedly curable by a mixture of black cumin seeds and oil. Many Muslims are great advocates of homeopathic medicine. Herbs, plants, seeds, and oils are commonly ingested for just about every ailment known to man. But I am not sure how Muslim theologians and doctors deal with this all-embracing claim for cumin. It is obviously not in agreement with grassroots realities or medical science.

Narrated Sahl: When the helmet of the Prophet was smashed on his head and blood covered his face and one of his front teeth got broken, Ali brought the water in his shield and Fatima (the Prophet's daughter) washed him. But when she saw that the bleeding increased more by the water, she took a mat, burnt it, and placed the ashes on the wound of the Prophet and so the blood stopped oozing out (4:98–99; 52.80.152).

This "remedy" for bleeding is to be found among certain rural Muslim peoples. Few if any credible doctors today would allow such treatment to be administered under his or her oversight.

The following is one of the more extreme examples of erroneous medical teaching found in the Hadith.

Narrated Abu Huraira: Allah's Apostle said, "If a fly falls in the vessel of any of you, let him dip all of it (into the vessel) and then throw it away, for in one of its wings there is a disease and in the other there is healing (antidote for it) i.e. the treatment for that disease."

[Translator's Note: Recently experiments have been done under supervision which indicate that a fly carries the disease (pathogens) plus the antidote for those organisms. Ordinarily when a fly touches a liquid food it infects the liquid with its pathogens, so it must be dipped in order to release also the antidote for those pathogens to act as a counter balance to the pathogens. Regarding this subject I also wrote through a friend of mine to Dr. Muhammad M. El-Samahy, chief of Hadith Dept. in Al-Azhar University, Cairo, who has written an article upon this Hadith. As regards medical aspects, he has mentioned that the microbiologists have proved that there are longitudinal yeast cells living as parasites inside the belly of the fly and these yeast cells, in order to repeat their life-cycle, protrude through respiratory tubules of the fly. If the fly is dipped in a liquid, these cells burst in the fluid and the content of those cells is an antidote for the pathogens which the fly carries] (7:452–53; 71.58.673).

The note is given as a scientific authentication of the treatment. Dr. El-Samahy is a theologian in an Islamic university. He is not a medical person. His reference to microbiologists as the source for his statements is unsatisfactory. Who are these biologists? Where do they teach? What are their scientific credentials? It is not proper to add such a note within the Hadith without giving authenticating documentation.

On the basis of this translator's note, I have heard an imam proudly proclaim that this Hadith has been pronounced accurate by the medical community. He made the statement with great gusto and dogmatism. To him the issue is settled. I find this type of blind faith sad and unsettling. It parallels the Muslim assertion that astronaut Neil Armstrong is now a Muslim and traveling all over the planet preaching Islam. No amount of rebuttals by Armstrong and others have yet put a dent in this unfounded rumor that has spread to the uttermost parts of the Muslim world. It would seem that even a face-to-face meeting between Armstrong and certain Muslims would be inadequate to make them realize the falseness of the statement. Their minds are set.

Narrated Anas: The climate of Medina did not suit some people, so the Prophet ordered them to follow his shepherd, i.e. his camels, and drink their milk and urine. So they followed the shepherd and drank their milk and urine until their bodies became healthy (7:399; 71.6.590).

Herein is an order from the Prophet himself. It was followed, with the result that those who drank the milk and urine of camels became healthy. This Hadith is repeated several times in the Al-Bukhari collection. It is not in the category of a disputed Tradition. I have never heard of a modern Muslim drinking camel's urine. It would be interesting to know how Saudis interpret this Hadith in light of the availability of camel urine in Arabia. One Muslim friend smiled sheepishly and told me such a commodity was not to be found in his country. I assured him it could easily be bottled and exported from Saudi Arabia.

> Narrated Urwa: Aisha used to recommend At-Talbina [a kind of porridge prepared from milk, honey, and white flour, etc.] for the sick and for such a person as grieved over a dead person. She used to say, "I heard Allah's Apostle saying, 'At-Talbina gives rest to the heart of the patient and makes it active and relieves some of his sorrow and grief.'" (7:406; 71.8.592–93).

Porridge is prescribed by the Prophet as an antidote to grief. There may be some value in eating an easy-to-digest, nutritious cereal at a time when one is emotionally distraught. But there is no proof that porridge will ameliorate one's mental condition.

> Narrated Ka'b bin Ujrah: The Prophet came to me during the time of Al-Hudaibiya, while I was lighting a fire underneath a cooking pot and lice were falling down from my head. He said, "Do your lice hurt you?" I said, "Yes," He said, "Shave your head and fast for three days or feed six poor persons or slaughter a sheep as a sacrifice" (7:406; 71.16.604).

Lice are a common problem in Two-Thirds-World countries. The simple treatment for children is to shave their heads. Adults usually solve the problem by applying medication to their hair. Ujrah was clearly told to shave his head. Then there was an additional dictum: fast for three days or feed six poor people or slaughter a sheep as a sacrifice. The questions arise when we try to understand the relationship of lice to fasting, feeding six people, and slaughtering a sheep. My only suggestion is to connect it to a cleansing procedure somewhat akin to what we find in the Old Testament. Lice defile, and these rituals offer a method of physical and spiritual purification.

Narrated Ibn Abbas: Some of the companions of the prophet passed by some people staying at a place where there was water, and one of those people had been stung by a scorpion. A man from those staying near the water, came and said to the companions of the Prophet, "Is there anyone among you who can do Ruqya [recitation of divine verses as treatment for a disease] as near the water there is a person who has been stung by a scorpion?" So one of the Prophet's companions went to him and recited Surat-al-Fatiha for a sheep as his fees. The patient got cured and the man brought the sheep to his companions who disliked that and said, "You have taken wages for reciting Allah's Book." When they arrived at Medina, they said, "O Allah's Apostle! (This person) has taken wages for reciting Allah's Book." On that Allah's Apostle said, "You are most entitled to take wages for doing a Ruqya with Allah's Book" (7:425; 71.34.633).

In Bangladesh I noted a professional fraternity of Muslim men who earned their living by reciting prayers for the dead. In the room where a corpse was lying, I once observed them haggling with a relative over the price for praying for forty days for the soul of the deceased. There was no real respect for these professionals who earned their salaries by praying. But the relatives felt obligated to fulfill mandatory religious rites. Also, Muhammad, according to this Hadith, put his imprimatur on the ritual of praying for the sick, a custom that extended to the deceased.

Actually, should we regard these men differently than we do any full-time worker who performs religious ministry for a salary? In reading a biography of A. W. Tozer, I get the impression that a significant part of his working day was spent in prayer. He was given a salary for this as well as his other activities. In any event, prayer is regarded by Muslims as efficacious for healing. This is in harmony with the teachings of most religions throughout the world.

Narrated Abu Huraira: Allah's Apostle said, "One should run away from the leper as one runs away from a lion" (7:409; 71.19.608).

There are significant contradictions in the Hadith concerning whether certain diseases are contagious or not. It is best to let Dr. Maurice Bucaille, a French convert to Islam, comment on these.

(There are statements in the Hadith) that diseases are not contagious. Al Bukhari's collection of hadiths refers in several places (chapters 19, 25, 30, 31, 53 and 54, Vol. VII, part 76, of the Book of Medicine) to certain special cases, e.g. leprosy (page 408), plague (pages 418 & 422), camel's scabies (page 447), and also provides general statements. The latter are however placed side by side with glaringly contradictory remarks: it is recommended, for example, not to go to areas where there is plague, and to stay away from lepers (Bucaille 1979, 246–47).

As the Prophet came to his final illness, we see the utilization of a certain style of healing.

> Narrated Aisha: Whenever Allah's Apostle became ill, he used to recite Al-Mu'awidhatan (i.e. the last two Surahs of the Quran) and then blow his breath and passed his hand over himself. When he had his fatal illness, I started reciting Al-Mu'awidhatan and blowing my breath over him as he used to do, and then I rubbed the hand of the Prophet over his body (5:510; 59.81.714).

This is a tender scene. Aisha, the eighteen-year-old beloved wife of Muhammad, is seeking to bring about the healing of her sixty-two-year-old husband as he lies on his deathbed. She remembered his method of inducing healing. She lovingly recited the Quran, blew her breath over his body, and then picked up his hand and rubbed it over his nearly lifeless form. All to no avail. The Prophet died soon thereafter.

I again quote Dr. Bucaille, who as a Muslim medical doctor is forced to note the lack of scientific credibility set forth in this collection of Hadith.

> We should not be surprised however to find that at a time when there were limited possibilities for the scientific use of drugs, people were advised to rely on simple practices; natural treatments such as blood-letting, and cauterization, head-shaving against lice, the use of camel's milk and certain seeds such as black cumin, and plants such as Indian Qust. It was also recommended to burn a mat made of palm-tree leaves and put the ash from it into a wound to stop bleeding. In emergencies, all available means that might genuinely be of use had to be employed. It does not seem—a priori—to be a very good idea, however, to suggest that people drink camel's urine (Bucaille 1979, 245–46).

Should we Christians acquaint our Muslim friends with the issues explored in this chapter? I find myself somewhat ambivalent in seeking to answer this question.

Yes, Muslims are scientifically vulnerable in a number of these citations. The Prophet simply echoed the wisdom of the age in which he lived. Many of these recommended practices are now known to be without merit. It is possible to undercut the authority of the Hadith by emphasizing these problem areas. Yet, is this an ethical approach? Do we not have some similar conflicts within the Old Testament law? At most, it is probably best only to ask for clarification rather than use such passages as a point of attack.

Potpourri of Teaching

*S*ince Islam is reputed to be a total code of life, it is therefore not surprising to find the Hadith touches on a myriad of subjects. This concluding chapter embraces teachings that are difficult to categorize.

Narrated Abdullah bin Umar: Allah's Apostle said, "When the Jews greet you, they usually say, 'As-Samu alaikum (Death be on you),' so you should say (in reply to them), 'Wa-alaikum (And on you)'" (8:181; 74.22.274).

This is a play on similar-sounding words, one of which means blessing or peace *(salamu)* and the other, death *(samu)*. In later stages of life, Muhammad became more and more opposed to Jews. He felt they had rejected him as a spokesman of Allah. From this Tradition it appears the feeling was mutual.

Narrated Abu Huraira: The Prophet said, "The young should greet the old, the passer by should greet the sitting one, and the small group of persons should greet the large group of persons" (8:165; 74.4.250).

Even such a mundane act as the proper format for exchanging greetings does not escape the attention of the Hadith.

> Narrated Aisha: Allah's Apostle came to my house while two girls were singing the songs of Bu'ath (a story about the war between the two tribes of the Ansar, the Khazraj and the Aus, before Islam). The Prophet laid down and turned his face to the other side. Then Abu Bakr came and spoke to me harshly saying, "Musical instruments of Satan near the Prophet?" Allah's Apostle turned his face towards him and said, "Leave them" (2:37; 15.2.70).

It is not clear whether "musical instruments" refers to the singing of the girls or to actual instruments. Islam has been ambivalent on the subject of music. Generally, nonreligious songs are loved and widely sung. There is no singing of any kind in the mosque, only chanting. But songs of the faith are quite common in special religious meetings and on the radio and television. There are, however, Muslims who oppose the use of any Islamic-generated music. In this Hadith Muhammad is allowing pre-Islamic songs to be sung in a home.

> Narrated Anas: When the news of the arrival of the Prophet at Medina reached Abdullah bin Salam, he went to him to ask him about certain things. He said, "I am going to ask you about three things which only a Prophet can answer: What is the first sign of The Hour? What is the first food which the people of Paradise will eat? Why does a child attract a similarity to his father or to his mother?" The Prophet replied, "Gabriel has just now informed me of that." Ibn Salam said, "He (i.e. Gabriel) is the enemy of the Jews amongst the angels." The prophet said, "As for the first sign of The Hour, it will be a fire that will collect the people from the East to the West. As for the first meal which the people of Paradise will eat, it will be the caudate (extra) lobe of the fish-liver. As for the child, if the man's discharge precedes the woman's discharge, the child attracts the similarity of the man, and if the woman's discharge precedes the man's, then the child attracts the similarity of the woman" (5:189; 58.49a.275).

Muhammad here invokes Gabriel as his source of information. The question can be raised as to why this revelation is placed in the Hadith instead of the Quran. Gabriel was purported to be

Allah's spokesperson for Quranic content. Perhaps Gabriel was said to be involved because of the nature of this test of Muhammad's prophethood. It was urgent that he produce credible answers. The first two responses point to future events and thus are not subject to scientific analysis. However, the third "revelation" from Gabriel is without medical credibility.

What follows is perhaps the most amusing Hadith ever published.

> Narrated Abu Huraira: The Prophet said, "The (people of) Bani Israel used to take their bath naked (all together) looking at each other. The Prophet Moses used to take his bath alone. They said, 'By Allah! Nothing prevents Moses from taking a bath with us except that he has a scrotal hernia.' So, once Moses went out to take a bath and put his clothes over a stone and then that stone ran away with his clothes. Moses followed that stone saying, 'My clothes, O stone! My clothes, O stone!' until the people of Bani Israel saw him and said, 'By Allah, Moses has got no defect in his body'. Moses took his clothes and began to beat the stone."
>
> Abu Huraira added, "By Allah! There are still six or seven marks present on the stone from that excessive beating" (1:169–70; 5.21.277).

Moses is a revered prophet in the religious teachings of Judaism, Christianity, and Islam. He is never ridiculed or demeaned. Yet, in this Tradition, Moses is seen running after a stone that is in the process of stealing his clothes. Upon apprehending the offending rock, Moses proceeds to inflict six or seven marks upon it.

All three religions affirm belief in the miraculous. But there is usually a major benefit or lesson to be derived from that which is supernatural. This story of a rock that is both animated and errant seems without application, other than it showed the Jews that Moses did not have a hernia.

> Narrated Abu Musa: The Prophet said, "A believer to another believer is like a building whose different parts reinforce each other." The Prophet then clasped his hands with the fingers interlaced (while saying that) (3:374; 43.6.626).

The ummah or community of Islam is of priority to Muslims. This Hadith highlights the importance Muhammad assigned to the supportive role each believer in Islam has one to another. Christian teaching is almost identical. The problem for both religions is in the practical outworking of such a lofty postulate. Strife and even violence within religious communities are a sad fact.

Narrated Ibn Umar: The Prophet said, "It is obligatory for one to listen to and obey (the ruler's orders) unless these orders involve one in disobedience (to Allah); but if an act of disobedience (to Allah) is imposed, one should not listen to or obey it" (4:128; 52.108.203).

This Hadith is generally compatible with the Christian position on submission to civil authority. If there is conflict with religious conviction, then obedience to God is to take precedence.

Narrated Abdullah bin Umar: Allah's Apostle ordered that the dogs should be killed.

[Translator's Note: The companions of the Prophet thought that this order was concerned with rabid dogs. Scholars differ as to harmless dogs, i.e. whether to kill them or not] (4:339; 54.16.540).

Back to dogs! Muslims have no love for dogs. This Hadith reinforces their bias, although one further Tradition makes pragmatic accommodation for keeping dogs.

Narrated Sufyan Ash-Shani: Allah's Apostle said, "If somebody keeps a dog that is neither used for farm work nor for guarding the livestock, he will lose one Quirat (of the reward) of his good deeds every day" (4:340; 54.16.542).

It seems there is something inherently unclean about dogs in the thinking of Muhammad. Otherwise why would a Muslim lose part of his religious reward for each day he keeps an unproductive dog?

Narrated Abu Huraira: Allah's Apostle said, "The Jews and the Christians do not dye (their grey hair), so you shall do the opposite of what they do (i.e. dye your grey hair and beards)" (4:442; 55.45.668).

Muhammad wanted to put distance between his followers and the Jews and Christians. Here is a specific, high-profile method of accomplishing that end. Older men are to dye their hair and beards. The color is not stipulated. My observation is that most Muslim men do not dye their hair, although some use black coloring and a few use red dye. There seems to be no legalistic ritual enforced in regard to this among contemporary Muslims.

> *"And We have Adorned the nearest Heaven with lamps"* (Quran 67:5)

Abu Qatada mentioning Allah's Statement said, "The creation of these stars is for three purposes, i.e. as decoration of the sky, as missiles to hit the devils, and as signs to guide travellers. So, if anybody tries to find a different interpretation, he is mistaken and just wastes his efforts and troubles himself with what is beyond his limited knowledge (e.g. To send a man over the stars or moon etc. is just a wasting of money and energy). (4:282; 54.3.420).

This seventh-century view of astronomy is religiously surrealistic. Did God create the heavenly bodies for decorative purposes? How are stars utilized as missiles to attack devils? On the other hand, they did have an elementary understanding of the navigational use of the stars. And there would certainly be those who would agree that it is a massive waste of money to send people to the moon or to Mars.

Narrated Abu Huraira: Allah's Apostle said, "Once Solomon son of David said, '(By Allah) tonight I will have sexual intercourse with one hundred women each of whom will give birth to a knight who will fight in Allah's Cause.' On that a companion of his said, 'Say: Allah willing' but he did not say, 'Allah willing.' Therefore only one of those women conceived and gave birth to a half-man. By Him in Whose Hands Muhammad's life is, if he had said, 'Allah willing', (he would have begotten sons) all of whom would have been knights striving in Allah's Cause" (4:56; 52.23.74a).

The Old Testament presents Solomon as having seven hundred wives and three hundred concubines. Extravagance in many areas of his life are well documented. But this incident is recorded in neither the Bible nor the Quran. There is no indication these one hundred women were his wives, although they may well have been.

Many readers will find it impossible to accept such a story. Solomon is depicted as having sex with one hundred women in one night. It is presented as historical fact, not conjecture or allegory. Then, because of his failure to say, "Allah willing," only one woman conceived. She subsequently gave birth to a child who was half human. There is no record of what made up the other half of the son.

The point of the story seems to be that Allah should be acknowledged in every detail of our lives. Solomon neglected to do so and therefore was disappointed in the results of his actions.

A Muslim will read this story with calm acceptance. Physical gratification is religiously restricted, but I have found that talking about sex is not. Perhaps Islam's societal restraints against fornication and adultery lead more to sexual fantasies on the part of Muslim men.

> Narrated Nafi: Whenever Ibn Umar was asked about marrying a Christian lady or a Jewess, he would say: "Allah has made it unlawful for the believers to marry ladies who ascribe partners in worship to Allah, and I do not know of a greater thing, as regards to ascribing partners in worship, etc. to Allah, than that a lady should say that Jesus is her Lord although he is just one of Allah's slaves" (7:155–56; 63.18.209).

Muslims deeply believe all Christians, by affirming Jesus as God, ascribe a partner to Allah. This then makes polytheism inevitable for Christians. Islam considers this as perhaps the greatest of all sins. It attacks the intensely monotheistic character of Allah. Jesus is not Lord but only a slave of God.

So then how could a Muslim man marry a Christian woman who holds to such a heretical and blasphemous view of Allah? This Hadith states that Allah has declared such marriages to be unlawful. In practice, however, these marriages are not at all uncommon. But a Muslim woman almost never marries a Christian man.

> No narrator: If, under compulsion somebody says about his wife, "She is my sister," there is no blame on him. The Prophet said, "Prophet Abraham said about his wife, Sarah, 'She is my sister.' He meant his sister in Allah's religion" (7:143–44; 63.10.193).

After observing Muslims for many years, I am brought to the conclusion that lying is not considered a serious sin. I have been told by Muslim friends that it becomes a sin if the consequence is bad. If lying does not harm, then it is not wrong. This Hadith, Muslims would point out, tells of an extreme situation in which lying saved Abraham's life. The lie was told under compulsion. Added to this Hadith is a rather remote rationalization. Abraham is said to have mentally added a phrase and declared Sarah to be his sister in the religion of Allah. I am not sure how the Hadith writer was supposed to know what was in the mind of Abraham.

> Narrated Ibn Abbas: Allah's Apostle cursed those men who similitude (assume the manners of) women and those women who similitude (assume the manners of) men (7:513; 72.61.773).

Muslim theologians uniformly denounce homosexuality as a major sin. There is to be a curse upon those who follow homosexual practices or even take on the mannerisms of the opposite sex. Through the years, I have done informal research on the subject in a number of countries. Also, in my reading, I have come across references to homosexuality among Muslims. The following are generalizations I have gleaned on the subject.

Lesbians are almost nonexistent among Muslims. Marriage is the norm for all girls, usually during their teenage years. This undercuts the potential for female homosexual activity. Also, girls would, at an early age, understand such behavior would not be tolerated.

Muslim men frequently marry in their mid-twenties or later. Premarital heterosexual experiences are prohibited for these young men. Muslim girls are tightly protected. This leaves prostitutes as one of the only options. In most Muslim countries prostitutes are available, though covertly. However, the other sexual option for men, particularly for the yet to be married, is homosexuality. Many are the documented stories of sexual relations between men. But the revelations usually come from Western sources, not Muslim. That is understandable.

Because of the social and religious stigma, Muslim homosexual men are careful not to take on female characteristics of any kind. No women's apparel or earrings are to be worn. Hand gestures are not effeminate. Hair length is not to imitate that of a woman. In short, they are maximally "closet gays." But word does get around. Straight Muslims denounce such sexual activity with ridicule and scorn. So, in every sense, homosexuality is aberrant behavior. Gays would rarely, if ever, be practicing Muslims. This is an important point to emphasize. There are many homosexuals among so-called Christians, but few of these are born-again, practicing believers.

There will be exceptions to what I have written. A great variety of cultural influences and practices exist among Muslims worldwide. Specific ethnographies could reveal more detail on a micro scale.

Narrated Abu Bakra: When the Prophet heard the news that the people of Persia had made the daughter of Khosrau their Queen (ruler), he said, "Never will succeed such a nation as makes a woman their ruler" (9:171; 88.18.219).

For many years I felt it was the macho spirit of Muslim males that made them unwilling to elect more than a token number of women to public office. Coming across this Hadith has helped me to understand their prejudice against female leadership. The Prophet himself has declared that a country ruled by a woman will not succeed. That is a serious prognostication for Muslim voters to ponder.

And yet, Pakistan and Bangladesh, with majority Muslim populations, have elected women rulers as either president or prime minister. They were functional heads of state, not ceremonial rulers. In these instances the ulama have loudly and vainly protested. Pragmatic politics have triumphed. The two highest female officials of their countries were both closely related to former rulers: Bhutto of Pakistan as daughter, and Zia of Bangladesh as wife.

A few Traditions highlight the Prophet's teaching on a simple lifestyle.

No Designation: The Prophet said, "Eat, drink, wear clothes and give alms without extravagance and without conceit" (7:454; 72.1.673).

Do Muslims follow the guidance of Muhammad? Some do, of course, out of necessity. Many of the world's poorest people are Muslims living in Islamic nations. What then about the affluent? Regrettably, I would conclude Muslims are like most of the rest of the world. Those who are wealthy live a lifestyle commensurate with their riches. Few voluntarily restrict their personal spending in order to share with the poor and downtrodden.

Narrated Abu Huraira: The Prophet said, "While a man was walking, clad in a two-piece garment and proud of himself with his hair well-combed, suddenly Allah made him sink into the earth and he will go on sinking into it till the Day of Resurrection" (7:457; 72.5.680).

Allah is presented as judging the proud man. Consistently, both in the Quran and Hadith, God is depicted as friend of the humble and the enemy of the proud.

Narrated Uqba bin Amir: A silken Farruj was presented to Allah's Apostle and he put it on and offered prayer in it. When he finished the prayer, he took it off violently as if he disliked it and said, "This (garment) does not befit those who fear Allah!" (7:466; 72.12.693).

Silk was the dress of the rich and powerful. For a short time Muhammad wore this cloth. Seemingly, during prayer he was convicted of its extravagance. His gesture of violence and declaration of its impropriety indicate he felt he had a word from Allah. The servant of God, he felt, should not dress richly.

Narrated Ibn Umar: Allah's Apostle wore a gold ring or a silver ring and placed its stone towards the palm of his hand and had the name "Muhammad, the Apostle of Allah" engraved on it. The people also started wearing gold rings like it, but when the Prophet saw them wearing such rings, he threw away his own ring and said,

"I will never wear it," and then wore a silver ring, whereupon the people started wearing silver rings too (7:502; 72.46.756).

The example of the Prophet was all-important to his followers. In this Tradition, the people commenced wearing rings when he did and took them off when he did. Apparently he felt gold was extravagant whereas silver was acceptable.

Narrated Abu Huraira: The angel of death was sent to Moses and when he went to him, Moses slapped him severely, spoiling one of his eyes. The angel went back to his Lord, and said, "You sent me to a slave who does not want to die." Allah restored his eye and said, "Go back and tell him (i.e. Moses) to place his hand over the back of an ox, for he will be allowed to live for a number of years equal to the number of hairs coming under his hand" (2:236–37; 23.67.423).

Once again we find Moses in an odd situation. Allah sent his angel of death to Moses. This angel was rebuffed by Moses in a most serious manner. God then intervenes and orders his messenger to go back and give Moses a plan for extending his life. The Hadith abruptly ends without indicating what Moses did. Why are these stories in the Hadith? Are they to be taken literally? Even though we may consider these accounts to be frivolous, are they that much more difficult to accept than the story of Job's encounter with Satan and God?

Narrated Aisha: A man said to the Prophet, "My mother died suddenly and I thought that if she had lived she would have given alms. So, if I give alms now on her behalf, will she get the reward?" The Prophet replied in the affirmative (2:266; 23.93.470).

Islam clearly teaches that Muslims should pray for the dead. They intercede for all the deceased prophets, including Muhammad. In this Tradition alms are encouraged to be given for those who have died. Through this intermediary effort, deceased Muslims will receive a reward, which probably means a lesser time of suffering for their sins.

Narrated Abdullah: The Prophet said, "He who slaps the cheeks, tears the clothes and follows the Tradition of the Days of Ignorance is not from us" (2:216; 23.37.384).

In pre-Islamic Arabia death was a time of great emotional outpouring involving self-flagellation and the tearing of one's clothes. Muhammad condemned such excesses as unbefitting to the new community of the people of Allah. They were to be restrained and to have faith in Allah who does all things well.

In practice, Muslims are much more vocal and extreme in their displays of grief at times of death than are Christians. The most intense outbursts of emotion I have ever seen at funerals have been those of Muslims. It would appear they do not follow the exhortations of the Prophet.

Narrated Ibn Umar: The Prophet said, "The deceased is tortured in his grave for the wailing done over him" (2:213; 23.33.379).

I am not sure why the deceased should be tortured for the sins of the wailers. Perhaps this was the Prophet's method of seeking to control the excessive outbursts of emotion that relatives and friends engaged in when their loved one died.

Narrated Aisha: Once Allah's Apostle passed by (the grave of) a Jewess whose relatives were weeping over her. He said, "They are weeping over her and she is being tortured in her grave" (2:212; 23.32.376).

How did Muhammad know the Jewish woman was being tortured in the grave? He claimed to have insight that passed beyond the normal perimeters of intelligence.

Narrated Um Atiyya: We were forbidden to mourn for more than three days for a dead person, except for a husband, for whom a wife should mourn for four months and ten days. (While in the mourning period) we were not allowed to put kohl in our eyes, nor perfume ourselves, nor wear dyed clothes, except a garment of Asb (special clothes made in Yemen) (7:193; 63.48.254).

It is interesting to note the excessively long period of mourning prescribed for a wife whose husband has died. This was to go on for almost four and a half months. But what was the mourning time for a husband whose wife had died? I tend to speculate it would be no longer than three days, if that. So goes the male attitude that permeates Islam.

> Narrated Amra: I heard Aisha saying, "When the news of the martyrdom of Ibn Haritha reached Allah's Apostle he sat with sorrow explicit on his face." Aisha added, "I was then peeping through a chink in the door. A man came to him and said, 'O Allah's Apostle! The women of Jafar are crying.' Thereupon the Prophet told him to forbid them to do so. So the man went away and returned saying, 'I forbade them but they did not listen to me.' The Prophet ordered him again to go (and forbid them). He went again and came saying, 'By Allah, they overpowered me (i.e. did not listen to me).'" Aisha said that Allah's Apostle said (to him), "Go and throw dust into their mouths." Aisha added. "I said, 'May Allah put your nose in the dust! By Allah, neither have you done what you have been ordered, nor have you relieved Allah's Apostle from trouble'" (5:393–94; 59.43.562).

The Prophet's aversion to emotional displays of grief is further amplified in this Hadith. He even goes so far as to order dust thrown into the mouth of the distraught women of Jafar. This seems rather cruel from our contemporary perspective.

> Narrated Aisha: When the last moment of the life of Allah's Apostle came he started putting his khamisa (blanket) on his face and when he felt hot and short of breath he took it off his face and said, "May Allah curse the Jews and Christians for they built the places of worship at the graves of their Prophets." The Prophet was warning (Muslims) of what those had done (1:255; 8.55.427).

Here we have Muhammad in his last earthly moments cursing Jews and Christians. How bitter he was against them to the very end. It is interesting to note his protest against worship at the graves of Jewish and Christian prophets. Yet, Muhammad's grave in Medina, Saudi Arabia, is probably the second most revered place for Muslims in all the world, the first being the Kaaba in Mecca.

And so the exalted Prophet of the desert died. His words and deeds, however, live on in the bosoms of more than one billion adherents of Islam throughout the world. To them, the greatest affirmation of faith ever to be penned or spoken is simply, "There is no deity except Allah, and Muhammad is his Prophet."

It is my prayer that this brief journey back through the centuries will help all of us who earnestly desire to understand Muslims as well as to introduce them to our Lord and Savior Jesus Christ. For readers who desire further input on how to share the gospel with Muslims I refer you to my earlier writings, particularly *New Paths in Muslim Evangelism* (Baker) and *Bridges to Islam* (Baker).

Glossary

Ablution: ritual washing before the prescribed daily prayers.

Abu Bakr: one of Muhammad's closest followers. Father of Aisha, Muhammad's favorite wife. He was the successor of Muhammad but only for two years. He died A.D. 634.

Abu Hurairah: one of the most constant attendants of Muhammad. He related more of the Traditions than any other individual. Died in A.D. 679 or 680.

Adhan: call to prayer.

Al Hudaibiya: a well near Mecca. Celebrated as the scene of a truce between Muhammad and the Quraish tribe.

Allah's Apostle: an honorific for Muhammad.

Anas (bin Malik): last of the companions of Muhammad. He died in A.D. 715 at age 103.

Ansari: the helpers of Muhammad. A term originally used for all followers of Muhammad from Medina.

Asr: the third, afternoon, prayer.

Bani Israel: the Jews.

Barakah: blessing.

Bilal: the first muazzin (caller to prayer) appointed by Muhammad.

Cupping: the process of extracting blood from one's body for medical reasons.

Day of resurrection: the last day, on which the bodies of the deceased are to be resurrected and judged by Allah.

225

Dhikr: corporate recitation of religious terms.

Fajr: the first prayer at dawn.

(The) Fast: the fast of Ramadan.

Fatima: the best known of the daughters of the Prophet.

Gabriel: the "divine messenger," the angel through whom Allah revealed the Quran to Muhammad.

Ghazwa: a military force led by either an apostle or an imam.

Hadith: the written collection of Traditions about what the Prophet said or did, or how he reacted to others. The Traditions were first transmitted by word of mouth.

Hafiz: one who memorizes the total Quran.

Hafsa: one of the Prophet's wives. The widow of Khunais, an early convert to Islam. Being the daughter of Umar, she had considerable influence in Muhammad's councils. She recorded several of his sayings.

Hajj: the pilgrimmage to Mecca.

Hajji, Hajja: one who has made the pilgrimage to Mecca.

Halal: that which is lawful according to Islam.

Haram: that which is not lawful according to Islam.

Hell (fire): the place of torment. It is said to have seven divisions or portals. "Verily, hell is promised to all together (who follow Satan). It has seven portals, and at every door there is a separate party of them" (Quran 15:44). Most frequently spoken of in the Quran and Tradition as an-Nar, "the fire." The word *Jahannam* occurs about thirty times.

1. Jahannam, the purgatorial hell for Muslims.
2. Laza, a blazing fire for Christians.
3. Al-Hatamah, an intense fire for the Jews.
4. Sair, a flaming fire for the Sabians.
5. Saqar, a scorching fire for the Magi.
6. Al-Jahim, a huge hot fire for idolaters.
7. Hawiyah, bottomless pit for the hypocrites (Hughes 1885, 171).

Hira cave: cave where Muhammad received the first revelations of the Quran.

Ibn Abbas: a cousin of Muhammad. Also called "The Interpreter of the Quran" because it is said that when he was ten years old the angel Gabriel appeared to him and revealed to him the meaning of the Quran. Died A.D. 687, aged seventy-two.

Ibn Sad: one of Muhammad's secretaries (wrote down the Quran as it was received by Muhammad).

Ijma: consensus of the community and ulama.

Imam: the one who leads the ritual prayer and is spiritual leader of the Muslim community.

Iqama: a recitation at the commencement of prayers when said in a congregation. A sign that all are lined up to pray.

Isha: the fifth, night, prayer.

Isnad: narrators of the Hadith.

Jihad: holy war. "Greater jihad" refers to a spiritual warfare against sin and all that is antithetical to Allah. "Lesser jihad" refers to the traditional interpretation of holy war against the opponents of Islam.

Jinn: spirit being. Jinn can be good or bad.

Jizya: tax taken from non-Muslims who are under the protection of the Muslim government.

Kaaba: cube-shaped building in the center of the mosque in Mecca that contains the Black Stone.

Kafir: one who disbelieves.

Kanz: treasure or wealth on which zakat has not been paid.

Khadija: first wife of the Prophet. She was wealthy and owned camel caravans.

Khaibar: place of a strategic battle in which Muhammad defeated his enemies.

Khamisa: a black woolen square blanket with marks on it.

Khutba: the sermon delivered at the mosque at the time of the Friday noon prayer.

Kuniya: calling a man, "O father of so-and-so," or calling a woman, "O mother of so-and-so." This is a custom of the Arabs.

Labbaik: "I stand and wait [at attention]."

Maghrib: the sunset, fourth, prayer.

Maimuna: last of the Prophet's wives. She was a widow, fifty-one years of age, when Muhammad married her. She survived the Prophet and died at age eighty-one.

Manumission: freeing a slave.

Matn: text of the Hadith.

Mecca: most holy city to Muslims.

Medina: second most holy city to Muslims. Place of Muhammad's grave.

Mosque: Muslim place of worship.

Muazzin: one who gives the call to prayer.

Muhram: person a woman can travel with (i.e., husband or person whom she cannot marry).

Muhrim: a Muslim intending to perform Hajj.

Mujahidun: men who fight in the cause of Islam.

Musalla: praying place.

Muta: temporary marriage.

Paradise: place of eternal reward for faithful Muslims.

Qadr: night in which the Quran was first revealed.

Qais: one of the Prophet's leading companions. He commanded the Prophet's bodyguard.

Qibla: niche in a wall of the mosque noting the direction of Mecca, towards which all Muslims must pray.

Quraish: the tribe from which Muhammad descended. For some time these people rejected the Prophet and were regarded as his enemies.

Ramadan: the month of fasting. Ninth month of the Muslim calendar. Also written as "Ramazan."

Rajm: stoning to death.

Ruqya: "enchanting." The word used in the Hadith for exorcism and incantation. Recitation of divine verses as treatment for a disease. The use of spells.

Safa and Marwa: two mountains near Mecca that the pilgrims run between during the Hajj.

Sahih: name given to the six major canonical collections of Hadith that came to be accepted by the Sunni community.

Salat: the liturgical form of prayer (five times a day). In Persian and Urdu it is "namaz."

Sauda: one of the wives of the Prophet.

Subhan Allah: holiness be to God.

Sunnah: the practices and way of life of the Prophet.

Surah: chapter of the Quran.

Shariah: Islamic law.

Tawaf: the march (circumambulation) around the Kaaba.

Tayammum: to put or strike lightly the hands over clean earth and then pass the palm of each on the back of the other, blow off the dust, and then pass them on the face. This is performed instead of ablution when water is not available.

Uhud: a hill about three miles from Medina. Scene of a battle where the Muslims were defeated by the Quraish in the third year after the Hijra.

Ulama: plural of imam. Spiritual leaders of the Muslim community.

Um: mother. Used in combination with other words it means "mother of," such as "mother of so-and-so."

Um Salamah: one of the wives of the Prophet. The widow of Abu Salmah, who was killed at the battle of Uhud.

Umar (Ibn Umar): the second Khaliph, who succeeded Abu Bakr in 634. He was assassinated in 644. He made the first collection of the Quran.

Umra: a lesser pilgrimage. It can be performed any time except during the time of the Hajj and omits the sacrifices performed during Hajj.

Zainab: one of the Prophet's wives. She was the divorced wife of Muhammad's adopted son Zaid (see Quran 33:37).

Zakat: almsgiving. The 2.5 percent offering. One of the pillars of Islam.

Zuhr: the second, noon, prayer.

Bibliography

Bucaille, Maurice. *The Bible, the Qur'an and Science*. Translated from the French by Alastair D. Pannell and the author. Indianapolis: North American Trust Publication, 1979.

Hughes, Thomas. *A Dictionary of Islam*. London, W. H. Allen and Company, 1885.

Kateregga, Badru D., and David W. Shenk. *Islam and Christianity*. Nairobi, Kenya: Uzima Press Limited, 1980.

Khan, Muhammad Muhsin. *The Translation of the Meanings of Sahih Al-Bukhari*. Arabic-English, Vols. 1–9. Beirut: Dar Al Arabia (P.O. Box 6089), n.d.

Khomeini, Ayatollah Ruhollah. *Sayings of the Ayatollah Khomeini*. New York: Bantam, 1980.

Nasr, Seyyed Hossein, "Sunnah and Hadith." In *Islamic Spirituality: Foundations,* edited by Seyyed Hossein Nasr, 97–110. New York: Crossroad, 1987.

Parshall, Phil. *Bridges to Islam*. Grand Rapids: Baker, 1983.

–––. *The Cross and the Crescent*. Wheaton: Tyndale House, 1989.

–––. *New Paths in Muslim Evangelism*. Grand Rapids: Baker, 1980.

Pickthall, Mohammed Marmaduke. *The Meaning of the Glorious Koran*. New York: New American Library, n.d.

Swarup, Ram. *Understanding Islam Through Hadis*. Delhi: Voice of India, 1983.

Wensinck, A. J. *A Handbook of Early Muhammadan Tradition*. Leiden: Brill, 1960.

Index